About *Creative Consciousness*

Doreen Maitre's *Creative Consciousness* is centrally concerned with the relationship between the Actual world and the 'Possible Non-Actual' of literature. She uses her life-long expertise in the philosophy of literature with great dexterity, but always wearing her learning lightly, and writing with limpid clarity and directness. Thought-provoking questions are posed with great force at the start of sections – 'Is there any real difference between an 'excuse' and a 'good reason' for individuals doing what they do?' she asks at the start of a discussion of issues of trust and betrayal in a novel set in an occupied country in wartime. Throughout, the emphasis is on the participatory engagement required of the reader, so that our own creating consciousness becomes a proxy protagonist in what we read, but always 'stepping aside' – 'aside' being what Emily Dickinson called 'slant' – from what we read. This is an important and engrossing book.

– Peter Barry, Professor Emeritus of English,
Aberystwyth University, author of
Beginning Theory and *Reading Poetry*.

The problem of consciousness and its relationship to understanding has preoccupied many writers over the last two centuries. Most concentrated on the mechanics of this relationship. Doreen Maitre's fascinating book, building on her earlier study of alternative worlds, gives the discussion a new twist, beginning with a survey of the levels and activities of consciousness, and of the identification and organization of the individuated self, and then moving beyond them to propose a moral function for consciousness as an essentially creative force which structures the individual's engagement, or lack of it, with others and with the world in general. Her thesis is illustrated by detailed discussion of literary texts as a means of showing some of the ways in which this engagement takes place, part of her argument being that literature is the crucial domain in which we can see most vividly what creative consciousness is and how it works in practice.

– Peter Washington was editor of the Everyman Library
from 1989 to 2008. His publications include *Madame Blavatsky's Baboon*,
The Future of Thinking (Routledge)
and *Fraud: Literary Theory and the End of English* (Fontana).

Doreen Maitre follows the tradition of Sartre and Merleau-Ponty in using literary and artistic creation to map the phenomenology of human mind and embodiment. She argues that our consciousness centres around a continual exploration of possible worlds; and that the writer's imaginative exploration is as potent a tool as the analysis and experimentation of science

for understanding our lived experience. This provides a readable and lucid account, drawing on close readings of various literary works, and it makes her book a worthy successor to David Lodge's *Consciousness and the Novel.*
– Steve Torrance, Professor Emeritus of Cognitive Science, Middlesex University; Visiting Senior Research Fellow, University of Sussex.

CREATIVE CONSCIOUSNESS

CREATIVE CONSCIOUSNESS
The Metaphysics of Lived Experience
and its Relation to Literature

DOREEN MAITRE

Greenwich Exchange
London

Greenwich Exchange, London

First published in Great Britain in 2021
All rights reserved

Creative Consciousness
© Dorren Maitre, 2021

Printed and bound by imprintdigital.com
Cover design by December Publications
Tel: 07951511275

Greenwich Exchange Website: www.greenex.co.uk

Cataloguing in Publication Data is available
from the British Library

Cover photo by Ben Harris © Ben Harris, 2021
www.benharrisphotography.com

ISBN: 978-1-910996-54-6

For K, Ben, Carol, Alex, Matilda with love

and in loving memory of Robert

ACKNOWLEDGEMENTS

My greatest debt of gratitude is to my former colleagues and students on the BA Literature and Philosophy degree at Middlesex Polytechnic / University who listened patiently to various early drafts of this book and offered extremely helpful comments and criticisms. Especial mention must be made of Keith Fleming, Marianne Korn, Jeff Mason and Peter Washington who were an unfailing source of stimulus and encouragement. David Conway rescued me from the Slough of Despond when I was flagging, with his painstaking and perspicuous comments and suggestions.

Further thanks are owed to my Philosophy Group in Dorset, an adjunct to my lectures for Bristol University (Department of Continuing Education). They faithfully continued the task of questioning my wilder claims and of offering their own valued insights into my subject matter.

My thanks also to Jeremy Hilton who patiently and thoroughly considered the manuscript and made a number of valued comments and suggestions for improvements.

My publisher, James Hodgson, was extremely hands-on and encouraged and advised me every inch of the way.

Infinite and ongoing gratitude of course to K, without whose assistance and support the book might never have been completed.

......

Thanks to Anthony Rudolf for letting me quote his 'Catalogue Sonnet' from *European Hours*, reprinted by kind permission of Carcanet Press Ltd, Manchester.

Quotations from the works of T.S. Eliot reprinted by kind permission of Faber and Faber Ltd.

Permission to reprint excerpts from David Miller's *Spiritual Letters* (*Series 1-5*) granted by the author and by the publisher, Chax Press; acknowledgements also to Contraband Books, who published an expanded UK edition of this work.

CONTENTS

PREFACE

PHILOSOPHY AND LITERATURE

THIS BOOK IS A SEQUEL TO my *Literature and Possible Worlds* (Middlesex Polytechnic Press, 1983) and an extension of some of the ideas explored there in an introductory way, as well as a more wide-ranging discussion of human consciousness 'as-lived'.

Since the earlier book, there has been an exponential growth of work on consciousness in several related disciplines – Philosophy, Psychology, Information Technology, Neuroscience – as well as a great deal more work on the interface between Literature and Philosophy, the two illuminating one another and yielding constantly unfolding new insights into human existence, such that Literature-and-Philosophy could now be considered a free-standing discipline of its own, encapsulated in the *Oxford Handbook of Philosophy and Literature* (ed. Richard Eldridge, OUP, 2009). One of the strengths of the new polytechnics, as they were called in the 1960s when they were set up, was their openness to the creation of new and exciting degree courses, combining hitherto separate academic disciplines. The BA Literature and Philosophy at Middlesex was one such, encouraged by Roger Waterhouse, Faculty Head of Humanities, who made it possible.

My stress will be on the implications of the creative, dynamic nature of consciousness, and I refer to material from a wide range of sources although my fundamental philosophical sources and starting points are Hume, Kant, Schopenhauer, Nietzsche and Scheler, whose insights into human experience have done so much to shape contemporary philosophical thought.

Contemporary thinkers who have informed my discussion are Antonio Damasio, Jonathan Glover, Bernard Harrison, Thomas Nagel, Martha Nussbaum, Peter Strawson and Charles Taylor.

However, the thought of individual thinkers is not discussed in detail, rather, there is a *distillation* of those aspects of their ideas which are pertinent to the main themes of the book.

My emphasis has changed from concentrating mainly on the role of imagination and possible non-actual worlds (PNAWs) in our understanding of works of literature to a more thoroughgoing analysis of *all* the activities of consciousness and the role they play in our attempts to understand ourselves, others, and the context in which we find ourselves. I hope that this will enrich our response(s) to works of literature and our deliberations about the nature of human existence.

I have tried to avoid the use of arcane philosophical jargon, so I hope the book will be accessible to a wide range of readers. A bibliography provides additional references and, nowadays, internet resources provide information for those wishing to pursue my subject matter in greater detail.

INTRODUCTION

CONSCIOUSNESS IS A NOTION OF SUCH complexity, discussed in several academic disciplines, each offering its own definition, that finding agreement is virtually impossible. Thus I will take my starting point by offering 'awareness' as a preliminary characterization of the phenomenon and then build up a fuller account in the course of this book.

The aspect I shall stress is the creative, dynamic one – consciousness is always 'on the move', throwing up incessant new material on the basis of which we attempt to make some sense of the world in which we find ourselves: an ongoing task. We seek certainty and continuity but are constantly 'On the edge of a grimpen, where is no secure foothold' (T.S. Eliot, 'East Coker', the second of the 'Four Quartets', in *The Complete Poems and Plays of T.S. Eliot*, Faber, 1969, p179).

The importance of works of literature to increasing our understanding of ourselves and our world cannot be stressed enough. Imagining, a central activity of consciousness, enormously expands the range of possible human experience by encapsulating possible-non-actual alternatives to actual lived experience, some of which may be actualised, as we shall see.

Along with a brief account of my methodology, I will outline what I see as the major metaphysical issues underlying or embedded in any discussion of consciousness. The rest of the book will pursue these in greater depth.

I have chosen to use the term 'metaphysics' because it encapsulates my aim to excavate the deep-seated organising principles embedded in our experience-as-lived, and to show the ways in which they contribute to our understanding.

Whether or not they are 'there' in any sense, or whether we impose them in order to make sense of our experience is an ongoing question, to which there can be no final answer.

Methodology

Analytic philosophy concerns itself with the analysis of concepts, the nature of argument on logical principles, and the discussion of such central notions as Truth, Meaning, Knowledge and Belief, as well as the structure of moral judgements. Its rigorous approach has provided an antidote to what some Anglo-American philosophers have seen as the maddening obfuscations of Continental Philosophy, eg Husserl and Heidegger, although others would argue that this is to throw the baby out with the bathwater so that, as Bernard Williams has observed, many of the important philosophical questions are 'off the page' (Bernard Williams, *Problems of the Self: Philosophical Papers 1956-1972*, CUP, 1973).

Analytic Philosophy held sway for most of the twentieth century and beyond in Anglo-American academia. In some cases, though not all, it moved into a preoccupation with Structuralism (eg Saussure, Lévi-Strauss) and Deconstruction (eg Derrida), although these were embraced with more enthusiasm by disciplines other than Philosophy, for example, Art History, English Literature, Film Studies.

Continental Philosophy, sometimes taken as synonymous with Phenomenology, in spite of the caveat mentioned above, *does* concern itself more directly with human experience 'as lived', and with attempting to describe the phenomena we experience without doing so by the imposition of any rigorous theoretical framework.

The distinction between analytic philosophy and Continental, while itself hard to draw with any clarity, still highlights a crucial divergence in their methodology. Analytic philosophy, to some extent modelling itself on that of the physical sciences, is suspicious of the notion of introspection, ie *first*-person accounts which are intrinsically *private* to the individual, and favours that which is *publicly* verifiable through *observation*; the most extreme version of this approach, also found in Psychology, is *Behaviourism,* which denies any role for first-person accounts and claims instead to be able to give a complete explanation of human experience through third-person observation, in line with explanations of physical phenomena in the Physical Sciences.

But, it can be argued, such an approach is *not* adequate for giving an account of consciousness, an intrinsically mental and private phenomenon, where what the individuals *themselves* consider their experience to be is of paramount importance.

The approach of this book may be considered to be roughly in the phenomenological tradition although I have tried to retain some of the rigour and clarity of analytic philosophy.

Two other approaches to the analysis of consciousness which I shall mention but not pursue in detail, are Artificial Intelligence (AI) and Cognitive Studies, and Neuroscience. What the methodologies of these approaches have in common is that they both provide *correlates* to immediate as-lived experience, correlates which often give rise to interesting and useful insights into our understanding of that experience.

AI involves the computer simulation of cognitive processes, including perception, decision making, and so forth. Margaret A. Boden's work on this subject is especially recommended.[1]

Neuroscience addresses itself to a study of the brain and nervous system and much has been achieved in this area in terms of explaining *how* the brain and nervous system functions.[2]

One aspect which emerges from this approach is the *therapeutic* in-depth study of the brain and nervous system involving detection of mal-functioning of the system and this can, in some cases, lead to treatment of it. This will be of particular interest to my discussion of 'the disordered individual' in later chapters.

---

[1] Boden is concerned with AI in relation to '*information-processing system(s)*': 'The computers, as such, aren't the point. It's what they *do* that matters.' (*Artificial Intelligence: A Very Short Introduction*, OUP, 2018, p3.) (For other valuable contributions to the discussion of AI, see for example Steve Torrance's articles in such journals as *Artificial Intelligence & Society* and *Philosophy and Technology*.)

[2] Antonio Damasio's writings are highly recommended in this context; see for example *Self Comes to Mind: Constructing the Conscious Brain*.

The Subject Matter of Consciousness

The subject matter of consciousness is experienced on three levels, the *actual* and the *possible* and the *transcendent*. It is usually claimed that what we take to be actual is what we experience through *perceiving* (through our *senses*), whereas what we take to be *possible* is that which *could* become actual but which remains 'in suspension' 'around' the actual. Such possible subject matter *may* become actual, or it may remain in its suspended state to be 'experienced' for its own sake *as* only possible. *Imagining* can be said to be the activity of consciousness which gives us access to this level or dimension of our experience, and it can be claimed that the Arts *par excellence* operate in this dimension. However, it is worth noting that a change of *attitude* can enable individuals to experience the actual in the same way as we experience the possible non-actual, by 'stepping aside' from being carried along by the importunities of *actual* existence. More will be said about this in later chapters.

Temporality: Transience and Transcendence

Let us consider for a moment this question of the importunities of *actual* existence. One of the key features of sentient life as-lived is that it happens *over time* – we are aware of constant *change* both in ourselves and in our surroundings, of moving from one state of affairs to another – relentlessly. It has already been mentioned above that some alleviation of this sense of 'hurry' may be achieved by imagining possible non-actual subject matter, and this is so, but, for some, there is a further dimension, problematically accessible, 'beyond' or 'outside' either the actual or the possible, which is timeless and 'objectless', and thus is free from the *transience* of usual human existence. To make this 'move' is normally said to 'transcend' it: for mystics and others (usually religious) the achievement of this state is sometimes claimed to be the goal or purpose of human existence, even if it is inaccessible to the more mundane.

> A mystic might
> discern hints of unworldliness –
> atemporal glints.
>   – R.A. Maitre, 'Mists', *Blue Barometers*, Peterloo Poets, 1986, p34.

Free Will and Determinism

After these preliminary remarks, we are getting closer to the nub of human existence as-experienced, to the essence that consciousness makes us aware of, and what role, if any, we have in the scheme of things. Are we merely the *recipients* of being alive among other entities, some living, some non-living, or do we play an *active part* in this scheme? The philosophical problem embedded in discussing this matter is that of Free Will and Determinism, perhaps *the* most important philosophical problem of all time: certainly a very prevalent one.

Another way of stating what is at issue is as follows: consciousness makes us aware that interaction with the world of entities (some living, some non-living) over time, makes 'things *happen* to us'; we grow and change and decay, as do other living entities, but at the same time, we would like to think that *we* can make things happen *to* our surroundings, including to other living entities. We would like to think that we formulate goals and purposes and intentions in the light of our appraisal of 'what is the case', and we pursue them because we *want* to, because we are *agents* rather than *patients*, at least some of the time. We can intervene in and change the direction of, or even stop, the remorseless movement of other entities, and mould it to *our* purposes. We would like to think that it is the possession of *higher* consciousness that makes this possible. However, ample evidence from the Physical Sciences claims that non-living entities and the *physical* dimensions of living ones behave in accordance with the cause-effect relations of inexorable physical laws – they have no 'say' in what they do. It is also argued that the non-physical or psychological dimension of *living* entities are likewise subject to determinants of which they are unaware, and hence have no ability to change or control.

The matter is unresolved and perhaps unresolvable.

The 'compatibilist' position, while acknowledging the undoubtedly determined nature of the operation of the *physical* world, suggests that the possession of 'higher' consciousness *does* make possible some measure of intervention and re-direction in what such entities 'do'.

This approach will be more fully explored in the course of this book.

It has been argued, famously by Freud, that below the level of *conscious* experience, lies a level of *un*conscious activity which *affects* our conscious experience but is *repressed* and thus unavailable *to* consciousness in intelligible form except by a trained analyst.[3] It is however possible to disagree with this, while not denying the existence of unconscious activity in, for example, the innocuous-seeming 'following a habit' where one is not aware of what one is doing because one is accustomed to it. The vexing questions are whether, or to what extent, if at all, we are *controlled* or *determined* by unconscious processes, and whether such processes can be 'brought to consciousness', and hence be controlled by *us*.

The debate about these questions, and more generally about free will and determinism, continues to rage and will be frequently referred to throughout this book. There is one matter where whether or not we have control of our lives, and hence can be *responsible* for what we do, revolves around the question of *praise and blame*. Certainly we assume that individuals *can* be held responsible for their actions – they are praised for 'acting well' and blamed for 'acting badly'. If they are *not* responsible for what they do because they are victims of uncontrollable unknown determinants, to praise or blame them seems unfair and unreasonable, but we do it nonetheless; although we are prepared, sometimes grudgingly, to accept that there can be 'exceptional cases' or extenuating circumstances. The possession of *self*-consciousness, the individual's ability to reflect on their own situation, *may* make the crucial difference.

Another current issue which I shall not pursue, except *en passant*, is that of Gender and Sexuality. At present this is receiving a great deal of hotly debated discussion, and the whole matter is so fluid that I do not feel I can add anything useful to it. In any case, I consider that the discussions of this book are relevant to *all* human beings, regardless of gender, sexuality, class, nationality, religion, because the underlying metaphysical concerns are universal.

---

[3] Access is available in dreams, for example, but they need to be interpreted in the right way, ie by someone skilled in psychoanalytic interpretation.

PART ONE
A DESCRIPTION OF CONSCIOUSNESS

1

THE ONTOLOGY OF CONSCIOUSNESS

1 THE FURNITURE OF THE WORLD

T HE WORLD IN WHICH WE FIND ourselves we experience *as* made up of, or 'furnished' with, myriad *individuated* entities, some resembling ourselves, others not. Some entities are non-living physical objects, others are *living* entities. It is an intrinsic 'given' of living entities that they strive to survive, that is, they seek food to sustain themselves and they seek to reproduce, thus propagating their *species* or group to which they belong. There is no ultimate explanation of *why* this is so, apart from the rather unsatisfactory one (to some) that 'God so willed it' or created things that way. However, there are many explanations of *how* this is so. The mechanisms of growth and reproduction have been very fully explored by Biology and Genetics so that we can now give reasonably full accounts of living entities and grade them in terms of complexity of structure and functions from the most primitive to the most sophisticated.

Living entities grow, change, decay and ultimately perish, some exhibiting movement or locomotion (animals), others not (plants), except for only limited 'movement'. Animals possess senses through which they are sensitive to and in contact with their surroundings via their nervous systems, which range from the most rudimentary to the very complex. At what point in this hierarchy *consciousness* enters the picture is a matter of debate. Some would say that the possession of a nervous system (brain and neural pathways) is the defining feature of conscious entities, in that such a system makes possible 'sensitivity' to the context in which the entity occurs: they exhibit responses to the stimulation of their senses; they are attracted or repelled by features of their context.

This crowded context (in which we find ourselves) is one of constant *activity* – we interact incessantly with other human entities, with non-human living entities and with non-living physical entities. It is a context of unavoidable *temporality*; we move from a past through a fleeting present, towards a future which never arrives completely because it is always succeeded by yet more futures *ad infinitum.*

Consciousness enables some living entities to be *aware* of this incessant activity, to *react* to it, and in some circumstances, to *change* its activity or direction. We may ask ourselves whether this activity is brought about *by* consciousness or whether consciousness is the mere *recipient* of it, that is, does consciousness *generate* its subject matter and activity, or does that subject matter and activity already *exist*, in some way 'waiting' to be made the subject matter of consciousness such that we recognise it *as* our experience? This is a fundamental question of metaphysics, one which can never have a satisfactory answer, but it lies behind or beneath all discussions of the nature of consciousness.

Another large question, equally hotly debated, concerns whether and to what extent, if at all, living entities possessing consciousness actually have any *control* of what happens to them. Are they merely the *vehicles* of self-contained physical and psychological systems which play out their operations in the context of living entities, or do (some) of those living entities (those with more complex nervous systems) have the ability to *intervene* in those systems, and *redirect* them?

If conscious living entities are 'merely' the vehicles of self-contained physical systems, does this make them 'merely' *spectators*, as it were, of those systems' operations, systems which operate through remorseless cause-effect relations with which the entity may become acquainted but be powerless to control?

Or, does this depend on the *complexity* of the relevant nervous system such that entities with complex nervous systems have the capacity to 'step outside' the physical cause-effect systems to which they are subject, *in order to* block, change, redirect them? If so, what is involved? This book will explore this possibility, and suggest that the possession of *self-consciousness* by the living entity may enable it to indeed stand aside from these remorseless cause-effect operations, to reflect on them, and perhaps at least in some circumstances to change or redirect them.

Why does this matter? Surely because the fabric of human existence is shot through with the notion of *responsibility*, that is, as stated above (in the Introduction), we praise and blame, reward and punish, one another for our actions, but that would be meaningless and unfair if the action in question was *caused* by a determinant over which the individual had no control. It would be unreasonable to say 'the buck stops here with you', if the individual concerned had no ability to 'do otherwise'. We shall return to this issue again and again, even if the conclusion/solution to the problem is only that we *must* proceed *as if* we have responsibility if human existence is not to be drained of all meaning.

2 ACTIVITIES OF CONSCIOUSNESS

Clusters or Nexuses of Interrelated Activities

One way of making a start on the analysis of the phenomenon is to talk of the *activities* of consciousness, ie what consciousness *does*, which comes a little closer to its fundamental feature: that it is active, dynamic, kinetic – our experience is of things 'happening'. We may not be clear in the first instance whether what is happening occurs 'outside' us, causing us to experience that external activity, or whether it occurs 'inside' us and is projected onto the 'outside', but trying to answer such questions is part of attempting to describe and explain what we mean by 'consciousness'.

Let us begin by saying that consciousness in general may be thought of as *sensitivity*, that is, that entities possessing consciousness are sensitive to stimuli, they are aware of what happens to them and *respond* to those stimuli. Whether they do this 'mechanically' as a plant turns towards the light, or 'consciously' as a human being takes offence as a result of an insult will depend on the type of sensitivity the entity possesses. Many people would argue that plants and the 'lower' animals do not possess 'consciousness', merely the ability to respond to stimuli in a 'blind' or 'mechanical' way. Only those creatures with a highly-developed nervous system can be said to be 'conscious', and this is because they alone have the capacity to 'deliberate' about how they might respond to stimuli, or even abstain from responding on occasion, based on some 'assessment' of their own situations. When we come to consider human beings we find that a key feature they possess is *self-consciousness*, ie not only the ability to respond to stimuli but also the ability to *reflect* on themselves and their circumstances – they are aware of themselves *as* entities among other entities, and have the capacity, to some extent, to *choose* how to react to 'what happens to them'. How is this possible? What can we say about *human* consciousness?

I have said that we are *aware* of ourselves as entities among other entities, and that we seem to have the ability to make choices about what we *do*. What does this involve? What capacities must human consciousness possess to make this a picture we recognise? The first thing to say is that human consciousness is a congeries of activities which interact constantly with one another to make human experience what it is, so that while it is unavoidable that they be discussed one at a time, no one operates in isolation from all the others, and 'operate' is the key term because they are all essentially active and dynamic. To be a human consciousness is to be constantly 'on the move', consequently I am adopting the present participle of each activity to try to capture their dynamic nature. These interacting activities are Imagining, Perceiving, Remembering, Feeling, Desiring, Willing, Reasoning, Judging and Communicating, and we are aware of experiencing all of these; and experiencing them makes human experience what it is.

Imagining, Perceiving, Remembering

What we call the 'actual world' is the context we experience through our *senses* and which we take to be the most 'real' and substantial state of affairs available to us. But at the same time, it is a feature of consciousness to experience many other 'possible worlds' which we can distinguish from the 'actual' world, but which nonetheless resemble it by comprising individuated entities standing in various relations to one another although these are not normally so 'well-defined' as those of the actual world. We usually call our experience of the actual world *perceiving*, and that of possible non-actual worlds as *imagining*, but this latter also includes *remembering*, ie experiencing that which *has been actual* in the past for the individual concerned, and is recognised as such – it is of *my* past experience. We now have to ask how these various worlds are to be distinguished from one another and the immediate answer is that it is a feature of human consciousness to be able to distinguish the one from the other ... normally.

Let us say something first about *perceiving*, the activity of experiencing through our *senses*. We consider that seeing, hearing, touching, tasting and smelling have an immediacy which other types of experience do not have, but there is more involved than this because these processes have *objects*, ie they are *of* something, and as a result of experiencing these 'somethings' through our senses we form a 'picture' of the object(s) in question. How does this occur? There must be more involved than 'merely' the stimulation of the sense organ, and the 'more' is that consciousness itself has the capacity to 'organise' or 'process' the sensory data to provide an 'image' of the object which has given rise to the sensory stimulation. But we are not aware of this process, we are aware only of experiencing objects 'ready-made' as it were, and of their existing 'outside' ourselves, or separate from ourselves, 'somewhere else' in the spatio-temporal field we occupy. But we are aware of a direct relation between the object and our experience of it, we take the object to be the 'cause' of our experience, and because of this we build up a picture of the world of our sense experience as being made up of various entities which *persist*, ie continue to 'be there' over time.

In addition to this we have the capacity to *classify* the entities of our sense experience according to similarities and differences between them – those which share certain characteristics we regard as belonging to one type, those which share other characteristics to another. Thus we learn that the world of our sense experience 'contains' a number of persistent entities of various types, and these are *physical objects*, and we too are physical objects in that we have a spatio-temporal persistence. But these physical objects do not all retain the *same* spatio-temporal location – they move about according to physical laws, as we do ourselves, and this motion and change is apprehended as occurring in response to or as a result of motion both within and between the objects. And persistent and regular motion and change is apprehended as *causation*, ie objects have the 'power' to affect one another, to bring about change, ie alternative states of affairs. Thus, without our apprehension of space, time, causation, regularity and recurrence we would not be able to 'make any sense' of our experience, or rather, we would have no recognisable experience.

Thus, the world in which we find ourselves has these features; this is the nature of our access to it, and this is the context in which we operate. But I have said that we also experience other 'worlds' than this one. What is their nature, how do we experience them, and how, if at all, do they 'interact' with the world experienced through our senses? The first thing to say is that these other 'worlds' which we may call 'possible non-actual worlds' are apprehended as having a different ontological status from the actual world – ie we *normally* 'know' that they are not the actual world, and this is because they have a number of features which make them differ from our sensed world. The most important of these is probably that they are not *shared* with other human individuals, ie are not publicly accessible, but are *private* to the individual experiencing them. One can get the agreement of another about the 'thereness' of an actual dog, but not of an imagined one. The other may grudgingly agree that one is experiencing an imagined dog if one describes it to them in detail, but they will not be experiencing it themselves, or at least not as a *publicly shared object*.

The more usual difference between the actual world and imagined worlds is that the latter are hazier; they have fewer contents and such contents as they have are less well defined than those of the actual world – normally. There are individuals whose imagined worlds are rich in content, and the content is very well defined, but these are the exception. Most imagined worlds are fleeting and elusive and lack boundaries so that in fact they can scarcely even be called 'worlds' – rather, they are collections of subject matter which we briefly experience and cannot retain at will, but the contents are normally recognisable as analogues of the subject matter of the actual world although they may be arranged in unexpected and unfamiliar conjunctions.

Our mode of apprehending imagined subject matter is different from that of the actual world: we are aware that it is not 'in' the actual world ie *external* to us, but rather, is internal to consciousness – indeed, has been 'created' by consciousness, sometimes from previously-experienced events and subject matter of the actual world, sometimes not. If the events and subject matter are recognised as having been actually experienced by the individual imaginer, we call the occurrence *remembering*, but this is nonetheless an activity of imagining, a special case of it, since imagining may be thought of as 'bringing to consciousness non-actual subject matter'. This is an activity of consciousness which is different from perceiving partly because the source of it is not the external world but 'within consciousness', and partly because the *range* of its subject matter is very much greater than that of the actual world. What we take to be the actual world is constrained by what it is possible to experience through the senses, which is itself constrained by the 'nature' of the actual world, ie what is physically possible. Imagined subject matter is not so constrained – it may consist of much which is physically *im*possible, although not incoherent ie unintelligible. Thus we could say that the actual world is surrounded by an infinity of possible worlds; and is itself a *precipitate* from the pool of possibility. Another way of putting this is to say that as physical objects are locked into the causal networks of the actual world they do not have the possibility of being otherwise than they are, but that imagining provides us with some access to the range of possibilities which could be, or could have been, or might be (in the future). It could well be that some of the imagined possibilities could never be actual because they contravene the physical laws which govern the actual world, but others could be actual in the future because they do not. Horses that can fly or humans becoming invisible might be given as examples of things that presumably could never be actual.

And so, what we experience via our senses is more limited than what we can experience through imagining. We can envisage future states of affairs which might become actual *for us*, as well as more general scenarios in which we may not be personally involved but which could nonetheless pertain in the future actual world. It is our awareness of this penumbra of possibility which has led much human thought and speculation towards the view that our physical here-and-now actual existence is but a tiny part of what *could* be experienced although there is considerable confusion about quite what status the 'could-be' might have. Certainly, without postulating the 'existence' of eg 'life after death', we already have experiential access to a great deal which is not actual because of the imagining capacity of consciousness, which enables us to move freely between the past, the future and the possible *by* imagining, and it is also important to realise that imagining plays a crucial and ineliminable role *in* our experience of the actual. Let us now say something about this.

We have said that our access to what we take to be the actual world – what 'really exists' – is via sense experience processed by consciousness which we call *perceiving*, and that the 'picture' we thus obtain is of a world of individuated entities standing in recognisable, regular, repeatable relations to one another which we call 'causal relations'. As a result of our recognition of these causal relations, we formulate 'physical laws', that is, the codification of such regularities which enables us not only to *infer* or *predict* future states of affairs but also, to some extent, to *control* them. This is the basis of scientific activity – the recognition of classes of entities possessing features which can be relied upon, in their interaction with members of other classes, to 'behave' in the future as they have in the past. Now, putting the matter in this way, we can see that the ability to engage in the identification and classification of entities and their interrelations is dependent upon our ability to 'hold in consciousness' previously-experienced entities and interrelations in order to make these judgments. If our experience was only of the present we would blunder around aimlessly, unable to identify anything with which we came into contact, and incapable of having any 'direction' because identification involves 'bringing to consciousness' previous experiences in order to make comparisons, and having direction involves the ability to envisage future states of affairs, and possible pathways to their achievement. Thus in fact our actual experience involves the ability to range over the past and the future in order to determine the nature of our *present* experience. And thus a great deal of non-actual subject matter must either be 'held in consciousness' or can be 'brought to consciousness' for there to be any actual experience that we would recognise.

It is not only our ability to envisage the future which aids the formulation of our purposes, but also that we can *remember the past.* We do so in order either to avoid remembered unpleasant experiences or to try to repeat pleasant ones, as well as contrive, as far as possible, states of affairs which have been useful to us. Without this ability to range over past and future in imagination we could plan nothing, and our 'activities' would be no more than blind obedience to survival-promoting 'urges'. What turns an 'urge' into a 'purpose' is our ability to reflect on it, to be *conscious* of it, and, in some cases, to do something about it.

The account given so far has been concerned only with our attempts to deal with and find our way about in the *actual* world – the world we apprehend through perceiving, although, as I have shown, our ability to do so would be impossible without constant recourse to *imagined* worlds. In fact, if one thinks through the implications of what has been said one cannot actually 'find' a 'present actual world' because, by the time one has reflected on 'the present', it has already become 'the past'. Nonetheless, our experience is *of* a persistent 'present' made up of continuities of objects and states of affairs which *persist over time* although they are all subject to *change*. Thus what we take to be present and what past is a somewhat arbitrary matter depending on the focus of our attention. If we attend only to what does persist and ignore its subtle changes, then we can claim that 'nothing has changed'. If, on the other hand, we do take account of what may be only subtle and minimal changes, then everything is in a state of constant flux with no stability and fixity.

However, in order to function at all in the context of what our perceiving apprehends, we ignore much of the change with which we are surrounded and act 'as though' at least *some* of the subject matter can be relied on to stay the same for all practical purposes. Thus it is that the perceived world is made up of persisting physical objects standing in persistent predictable relations with one another intermingled with a great deal of subject matter which has a far more elusive and problematic status. My computer, my desk and my bookshelves have recognisable qualities which can be relied on to stay 'there' over time but my thoughts, feelings, tastes and values are far more fugitive and difficult to define or 'capture' because they are not 'anywhere' in the sense of having a spatio-temporal location; all one can say is that they are loosely 'associated' with my physical body, but the nature of the association is very difficult to specify because they are features of my consciousness, not of my physical body. Nonetheless, one would want to claim that they *exist* as much as my desk exists, but it is certainly a different mode of existence from that of physical objects. Insofar as thoughts and feelings etc are experienced, and they certainly are, then they exist for consciousness, and because one cannot talk about them in the same way as one discusses physical objects is no good reason for suggesting, as sometimes occurs, that they have a 'lesser' status from that of such objects.

At this point it might be worth introducing a useful metaphor from the physical sciences – that of 'suspension and precipitation'. The *precipitate* is a solid emerging from a *solution* or from a *suspension*. I have already mentioned that one could regard the actual world as a *precipitate* from the infinity of possible worlds which surround it, and now is the time to say a little more about this because it is an illuminating analogy. When a substance is 'in suspension' in a liquid it is dispersed throughout it in a 'fine' and expanded form; but it can change its form as a result of a chemical reagent and becomes heavier and more condensed so that it sinks to the bottom of the vessel as a solid form or precipitate. The relevance of this to the actual/possible world relation should be obvious: possible worlds are less dense, more fluid, in suspension 'above' or 'around' the actual world. But when a possible world becomes actual it becomes denser, less fluid, more solid, precipitated, and this is the form in which it is accessible to *perception*. Possible worlds are accessible only to *imagination*. What is the 'reagent' which brings about a change of state? It could be the activity of consciousness in 'actualising' it, ie in bringing about some future possible state of affairs; alternatively, it could be that 'it just happens' as a result of actual states of affairs following their causal pathways. I suggest that both occur, and that the actual world of physical objects changes in the latter way while, as a result of the *intervention* of human consciousness, states of affairs which would *not* otherwise occur, can be made to do so.

Thus, the ability to imagine possible non-actual states of affairs is a crucial part of bringing about future possible states of affairs in the actual world, and this is an activity of human consciousness, and one which can be regarded as illustrating its *creative* nature. I have already said that without the intervention or contribution of human consciousness, much which occurs in the actual world would not do so – we can imagine the physical world carrying on perfectly well without us (perhaps better!), we are not necessary to its functioning, and we know that it functioned for countless millennia before the emergence of human beings – so that our effect is something over and above what would 'naturally' occur, and one could say that we 'design' new configurations of subject matter. Certainly the 'raw material' used in such designing is that which is already available to us but we 'work' it in ways which 'nature' would not, and produce new subject matter as a result. Just as an artist 'works' with paint and canvas to produce a painting, or a carpenter uses wood to make a table, so human consciousness shapes the contents of the actual world for its own purposes, making use of the given qualities of the 'material' to fulfil its own designs. These designs may be extremely hazy and ill-defined, but we have *some* idea of what we want to achieve, albeit in the very short term much of the time.

What has been said so far relates to our access to and participation in the *actual* world, and this is certainly an essential aspect of human experience given our embodied physical nature. While the possession of self-consciousness enables us to be aware of, reflect on, and act purposively in the actual context in which we find ourselves, it is not the only role played by imagining in human experience. In addition to contributing to our understanding of the actual world in the sense of enabling us to 'find our way about' in it, imagining also makes it possible for us to a.) take a different attitude to our actual experience from the participatory one, ie that of a spectator or observer, and b.) to create and explore possible non-actual worlds 'for their own sake', rather than attending primarily to their potential for actualisation. Let us now say something about these two additional activities or capacities.

Participants and Spectators (*Reflective Attitude*)

This first function of imagining is sometimes known as the 'aesthetic attitude' but I think this is a rather misleading term, suggesting as it does that one is attending to the 'sensory' dimension of the subject matter under consideration, rather than to its relational aspect ie in what relation the object stands to other objects, and what *practical* purpose it might serve. Some of the points that are made about aesthetic experience are useful to us but only some of them, so I will not persist in using the term 'aesthetic', but rather will talk of the difference in attitude and its attendant experience between being a participant and being an observer or spectator. Our primary response to the perceived world is one of *involvement*: as sentient, embodied, vulnerable beings we apprehend ourselves as possibly 'under threat' from our surroundings, both from non-living matter and from other living beings, non-human and human. In order to survive (and this is a 'given' imperative of all living beings for which there is no additional explanation) we need to have as accurate a picture as possible of what our context contains, and a number of strategies for pursuing what enhances our survival and avoiding what threatens it.

We have seen that, while imagining plays a crucial role in this, it is at the service of the primary aim ie to survive, and one may say that if this is the object of one's attention, then one has a *practical* attitude, one is concerned with what needs to be *done*, with negotiating one's way around the actual world. In other words, one is attending to the causal imperatives and importunities of the physical world because eg if one does not eat one will die, and if one does not avoid predators one will perish.

Thus, life on the practical level involves one in 'keeping one's wits about one'; if one doesn't one is likely to run into trouble unless someone else is looking after one full-time, something which does not occur very frequently after childhood, except for the lucky few! The rest of us have to learn, by a mixture of personal experience and the advice and guidance of others, to fend for ourselves. The physical dimension of the actual world is *difficult* to negotiate so that we need to be as clear as possible about what is what, and this means that for many people life is lived only on the practical level. However, it *is* possible, at least some of the time, to apprehend it in another way, ie to respond to it in a contemplative or reflective way as an observer rather than as a participant. This mode of apprehension is sometimes described as 'timeless' in that one feels a temporary release from the demands of the 'here and now'; one can ignore the need to satisfy one's primary survival-enhancing desires and attend to the 'design' of actual subject-matter as one attends to a work of art, that is, 'for its own sake' rather than in order to satisfy some practical demand.

It could be that such a release is spontaneous – one's attention is captured by a stunning sunset – or that one contrives it by a deliberate 'flip' from the practical to the contemplative attitude. Surely everybody experiences such spontaneous releases from time to time, but a deliberately willed change of mode of apprehension is less frequent and more difficult to effect, especially in western society where such 'escapes from reality' are discouraged. We are taught to attend to the nuts and bolts of the actual world in order to 'get on' and achieve all manner of practical tasks which, we are told, are necessary for our survival. Certainly some of them are, but others are not, and the imperatives of 'work' resulting in large measure from the so-called 'Protestant Work Ethic' can be seen as unnecessarily artificial, going, as they do, far beyond the requirements of 'mere' survival. It is a constant jeremiad of critics of Capitalism that it encourages people to 'need' far more material goods than they know what to do with, or can genuinely appreciate.

This may or may not be so; what is clear is that incessant preoccupation with the practical discourages the contemplative mode; and the irony is that release from mere-survival demands makes it far more possible to appreciate the actual world in a non-practical way. Whether doing so is regarded as worthwhile will depend on people's ability to attend meaningfully to actual subject-matter 'for its own sake'. What is to be understood by 'for its own sake'? I have said that it resembles the attention one gives to a work of art, ie that one responds *as-if* the actual world is a work of art, and because of this way of putting the matter, this mode of apprehension is often called 'aesthetic', although here we will be using the terms 'reflective' or 'contemplative'.

What is there to be said about the reflective apprehension of the actual world; what is it to apprehend it as-if it were a work of art? We have already said that we are not concerned with the practical significance of the subject matter in the sense of asking what *use* it is to us in solving some practical problem we have, and in addition, because of this, we can attend to features of the subject matter which normally we would ignore. We are not even concerned to *identify* it because to do so is part of making a map of the actual world, of *locating* subject matter relationally, ie in terms of how it stands in relation to other subject matter: we ask, 'is this an X or a Y?' because we need to know in order to find our way around. Kant's distinction between practical and aesthetic modes, with the example of attending to a plant (say, by a botanist or an artist), can be found in the *Critique of Judgement*. The botanist, unlike the artist, seeks to *identify* and *classify* the plant, ie to place it under a *concept*. But with reflective apprehension we are not trying to find our way around, we are 'at rest' in the sense of being observers or spectators. Just as we are not required actually to 'take part' in a film we are watching, or in a novel we are reading, so we can 'stand on the sidelines' of actual events and observe them – we do not take responsibility for them.

It has already been pointed out that the way we classify the subject matter of our perceiving is by noting *shared* features of individual entities and grouping them according to these features, and that in this way we are able to identify an entity as being a member of a particular class, or an example of a type. And when we do this, we 'leave behind' or ignore features which are *not* shared, and which give the entity unique individuality. Now it is this unique individuality we can attend to when our aim is contemplative or reflective rather than practical, and the consideration of an entity in this way reveals new features (and relations) which otherwise go unnoticed. Our primary concern is with the uniqueness. What is the point of this concern with uniqueness? In the case of a work of art, our appreciation of it is enriched by acquainting ourselves with all its features, not just those which have practical significance, and this is a source of satisfaction. In the case of the reflective apprehension of the actual world the same applies – we become acquainted with the richness and diversity of its subject matter, likewise a source of satisfaction; and also, briefly, because we are absorbed in subject matter with which we have no primary practical concern, we are released from the demands of the practical, experienced as often as not as tiring, tiresome and unpleasant.

This last claim may come as something of a surprise but it is of the utmost importance. One of the key features of human beings which receives very little philosophical attention, is that they get *tired!* And they get tired because they are embodied living things which require a great deal of energy to 'keep going', and the primary source of this energy is *food* which must be acquired at frequent intervals, and without which they perish. This is so obvious that its significance is usually overlooked. We shall see that human beings are being constantly 'pulled' by their desires, and that the satisfaction of these desires requires *effort*. Now, that which requires effort, requires energy, and energy requires fuel ie food (and drink), and we know that for vast numbers of humans the search for sustenance has taken up almost all their time and energy, and still does for many of them. Thus any release from the survival imperatives is experienced as pleasant – resting, sleeping, dreaming, and reflectively contemplating the surrounding subject matter without the need to *do* anything about it.

But is there any other point to such reflective contemplation of the actual world over and above the fact that it provides a 'break' from involvement in practical tasks? The answer is that there certainly is, because noticing features of subject matter otherwise ignored *changes* the view we have of the actual world, and this in turn contributes to enriching the 'map' we have of it which we use to 'move about' in order to satisfy our desires and achieve our purposes. As the result of such contemplation we may come to value some objects and events more highly than others, and consequently amend our plans and aims in the light of doing so. This ability to give serious attention to subject matter 'for its own sake' rather than in terms of its relational practical function is central to the argument of this book, because I shall be arguing that the expression and articulation of unique individual potential must be a prime value of humanity if there is to be any hope of it organising itself in a better way than hitherto. All I want to establish at present is that this ability or capacity to attend to *differences* already resides in human consciousness but is misused, or perhaps, underused.

We may see that failing to value the contents of the actual world results as much from an inability to give real contemplative attention to them, seeing them rather merely as means to some future end, as from the intrinsic wickedness of human beings; although the results may be identical. Whether millions of people are made to suffer and die is the result of a malignant enjoyment of inflicting pain or is the outcome of an inability to appreciate the intrinsic worth of other human beings, regarding them as sub-human, makes no difference for the victims, but it makes an enormous difference to our reflections on such atrocities. If we regard such behaviour as an ineliminable feature of humanity, as 'original sin', then we are less likely to make any attempt to do anything about it than if we see it as something which *can* be at least minimised by encouraging people to appreciate the intrinsic worth of other human beings (and, by extension, of all living things), through attending to the *uniqueness* of individuals. I am not suggesting that this can be achieved by reflective contemplation *alone*, only that the development of this capacity can *contribute* to doing so. There are many more stages in the argument before we can have any reasonably full account from which we might draw some conclusions.

Suffice it to say at present that this mode of attention is already available to us although its employment is discouraged by many of our current aims and values. It is not *just* that it provides a welcome relief from survival demands – although it does – but also that it has a far more positive role in human consciousness, that of enabling us to acquaint ourselves in greater depth with the subject matter of our experience. Of course this does not necessarily mean that we are going to find all such in-depth acquaintance *pleasant* or worthwhile; on the contrary we may find much of it distasteful in the extreme – a close appraisal of the sufferings of a torture victim, for example – but this is my point; the increase in *sensitivity* brought about by reflective contemplation *could* mean that such practices come to be regarded as totally intolerable and unacceptable. Of course, this will depend on the 'goodness of heart' of the individual contemplator, and I shall have something to say about this in a later chapter.

We are now in a position to ask what role *imagining* plays in this mode of attention, and this is an interesting question because so far we have talked of imagining as being concerned with possible *non-actual* subject matter, and perceiving with the actual world, yet in this case we *are* concerned with the actual world but in a *different way* from our 'normal' stance or orientation towards it. Is this imagining or perceiving or some hybrid of the two? Certainly it shares some features of both – the subject matter is *actual* but our mode of attention is such as to treat that subject matter *as-if* it were possible non-actual by distancing or detaching ourselves from *some* of the features of the actual world, ie the relational and causal aspects. Our primary concern is *not* to identify or classify it, nor to attend to its spatio-temporal relations with other subject matter, nor to be interested in the causal networks of which it forms a part, although all of these may have *some* relevance to the experience. A way of putting this might be to say that, as it were, we *lift* the subject matter out of its spatio-temporal causal context and attend to it *in isolation* – we ignore the context in which it *actually* occurs.

Let us take a simple example to illustrate this: consider the lamp-post in front of my house, identical, for all practical purposes, with several dozen other in my road. I admit that I have never given it a moment's attention apart from taking care to avoid it when walking down the road, or perhaps noticing a man up a ladder repairing it. I suppose I notice it when it is not working but that is all. If I now engage in a deliberate 'flip' in order to attend to its intrinsic properties, I notice for the first time that it is a fairly uninspiring concrete column with a single light at the top. I suppose I could find some merit in the fact that the column is slender and curves quite elegantly at the top to focus the light on the road rather than the pavement (is this a good thing?!) but otherwise there is little more to say. Close perusal of the column might reveal that the concrete has an interesting texture and colour – this is the sort of thing a painter would perhaps tell one to do – and I could attend to the light it gives and the shadows it throws at night. In fact, with a bit of effort I could get quite interested in that lamp-post, and just writing about it has made me realise that it compares unfavourably with other, neo-Victorian lamp-posts in more tourist-visited parts of the town, and I wonder if the local council could be persuaded to install them here.

Trivial as this example is, it serves to illustrate a number of the points I have been discussing, namely, that even in the case of the most common everyday objects of the actual world, unless one makes a special effort one does not notice them at all; that when one does make the effort one 'sees' far more detail than one otherwise would; that as a result of so doing, one makes a number of new judgements (why not neo-Victorian instead of utilitarian concrete?). It should now be obvious that if one transfers this mode of attention to other, more serious subject matter of one's actual experience, one is going to 'see' far more than one otherwise would, and that this could result in a modification of one's views about all manner of things. The unoriginal analogy which comes to mind is that of a horse wearing blinkers – if we attend only to what is of practical importance to us we are likely not only to misidentify it but also to act in ways which we would not if we had a richer contact with the actual world. Certainly the blinkers of a practical approach seem to make human experience *simpler* – while we do not 'see' a good deal of the richness of things we also avoid 'seeing' a good deal of its horror – so the question is whether or not this is too high a price to pay for 'a quiet life'. Much of this book is concerned with this question.

While discussions of the reflective attitude often concentrate on the *visual*, it is worth noting that it could and should also apply to the auditory, the tactile and the olfactory. Focusing our attention on sounds, 'feels', tastes and smells also enriches our appreciation of the actual world. Gourmets focus on their food, wine-tasters on their wine, musicians on sounds.

Imagining for Its Own Sake

Let us now say something about imagining which is not concerned with our experience of the actual world. This is what is normally thought of as imagining-proper: the creation and exploration of possible non-actual subject matter as a source of interest and feeling without the aim of actualising it. Our most casual daydreams may be of this nature, although frequently they contain a component of 'if-only', that is, we would like what we imagine to become actual, although we may have little hope that it will do so. However, the content or subject matter of such daydreams is usually hazy, ill-defined and incomplete, and of short duration. We dream of the day we will retire, or of discovering that we are suddenly rich, or of winning the Nobel prize, and skate about over a number of sketchy scenarios which might be involved in these things happening but do not pursue any of them in any detail. We may find such daydreams absorbing and provocative of considerable emotion; we may return to them again and again without filling in many details, and we may, if we are sensible, consider the disadvantages of such states of affairs becoming actual, thus reducing the sense of frustration and longing which may accompany them.

But daydreams are largely unstructured: the subject matter may change from moment to moment, or be quite different if the dream is repeated without any feeling of dissatisfaction, so that one can scarcely talk of possible non-actual *worlds*, rather thin slices of such worlds, where we are not conscious of many of the relations in which the experienced subject matter may stand 'within' such worlds. However, by an act of will, far more structured possible worlds can be created by human consciousness; we can deliberately persist with filling in the subject matter so that our imagined world becomes 'peopled' with a richness and complexity approaching and resembling that of the actual world. Why should we bother to do this? Reasons vary; it may be that our actual existence is so boring and uninspiring or painful that we prefer to spend our time among the subject matter of our imaginings, so much so, that such worlds constitute a parallel 'life' for some individuals. Or it may be that we find satisfaction by expressing our imaginings in an externalised form such as a novel, where the act of writing itself provides a stimulant to the imaginings. This is a very widespread activity arising from a number of different motivations, from the need to earn money to the desire for literary fame. Whatever the motivation, the activity itself certainly involves the creation and exploration of highly structured possible non-actual worlds but in this case, instead of remaining private to the individual, they acquire a public dimension through the medium of writing.

Now, the experience of such worlds, like our experience of the actual world, involves *feeling*, but not in quite the same way. I have already said that when we explore possible non-actual worlds their subject matter may arouse in us feelings of eg frustration and yearning because we wish them to be actualised, but this is over and above what we feel about the subject matter *itself*. Supposing I imagine a possible non-actual state of affairs in which I embark in walking round Britain on the coastal paths, what would my imagined experience be? I would feel excited at the prospect, daunted by its magnitude, fearful of being fastened on by tiresome fellow-walkers, apprehensive of having an accident, hopeful that a close friend might accompany me. All these feelings would flit through my consciousness, approximately related to the relevant subject matter but they would surely be experienced with *less intensity* than if I was actually taking the walk – they would be pale analogues of actual feelings, ie feelings experienced in the actual world. Or would they? I think the answer is, not necessarily; it depends on the individual imaginer and on the specific imagined subject matter. There can be enormous variation in the intensity of the feelings experienced in connection with imagined states of affairs, and this is sometimes related to the detail of the subject matter, sometimes not.

It might be thought that if one 'fills in' the details in one's imaginings this would increase the intensity and vivacity of the associated feelings, and while this is sometimes so, it is also the case that a mere fleeting image can be enough to arouse the most violent reaction. Thus there is more involved than the detailed clarity of the subject matter – an important component of the experience is the *significance* of the subject matter for the individual imaginer. A nervous individual may shake with terror about an imagined situation which would seem of the utmost triviality to another; a 'nerveless' person may be able to contemplate with equanimity what would seem to most of us to be a petrifying possible state of affairs. This observation is of the utmost importance in interpersonal relations and I shall be discussing it further in Chapter Three.

Day-dreaming, as it is called, has already been discussed as a variety of the creation of and access to PNAWs, but what of *night*-dreaming, something which we all do?

In mythology, some sacred texts, notably the Bible, and the belief systems of many cultures, it is regarded as highly significant, sometimes for its *predictive* powers: it is thought that the content of dreams enables us to 'see into the future', and hence to act in accordance with it.

In modern times, Freud, famously, argued for their revelation of deep-seated, otherwise repressed preoccupations of the dreamer, although the ingenuity of the 'interpretations' may stretch credulity.

Certainly, dreaming is a source of inspiration to many writers and artists, and writers such as J.W. Dunne (*An Experiment with Time*) and J.B. Priestley (*Man and Time*) suggest that dreaming has a significance beyond the mere activity of the mind 'at play' when we lose consciousness.

For the purposes of this book, we can say that dreaming is yet another source of PNAWs, although sometimes brief, unstructured, puzzling ones, or sometimes not, but often bearing an unsettling similarity to actual experience. Responses vary from a brisk dismissal to the attribution of significant, life-changing meaningfulness according to the vivacity or paucity of its subject matter.

In addition to the actual and the possible, there is another ontological level with which consciousness operates and this is the *Transcendent*, as already mentioned. Sometimes regarded as the preserve of mystics and religious people, it is nonetheless available to all, though only hazily. Its main feature is that it *lacks* features – it is 'outside' the spatio-temporal and contains no subject matter. Nonetheless, it is thought by some to give us access to the 'really real' which lies behind or beyond our 'normal' experience. For an in-depth discussion of this, see R.C. Zaehner, *Mysticism Sacred and Profane.*

Feeling, Desiring, Willing

The two thinkers who most inform this discussion are the 19th century German philosopher Arthur Schopenhauer, in connection with the pre-eminence of Desiring, and Antonio Damasio for his work on the close interaction of Mind and Body, as well as Brian O'Shaughnessy for his definitive work on the Will.

For Schopenhauer the incessant welling up of unsatisfied desires is a source of dissatisfaction and suffering, something to be rid of or escaped from, in his case by embracing some form of transcendence. Schopenhauer is regarded as the arch-pessimist; but I suggest that a more positive account of desiring may be possible.

Human consciousness is unavoidably associated with *embodiment.* I do not intend to discuss the nature of the association over and above saying that human beings are *feeling* entities, ie ones which have the capacity for pleasant and unpleasant experience which, in the first instance, comes to them via their *senses.* Our bodies are such that we experience pleasure and pain by means of our nervous systems according to the nature of the stimulus, which may be 'external' (from outside the body) or 'internal' (from within the body itself). In addition, we experience positive or negative feeling which does not seem to be directly related to bodily sensation although it may have physical concomitants, and which is 'directed towards' some object: and this we call 'emotion'. Within these two basic types of Feeling – the physical and the non-physical – there is a large range of sub-divisions: we speak, for example, of aches and tickles and spasms and shudders within the first, and of anger and fear and love and hate and boredom and indignation within the second. (These are very thoroughly explored by Gilbert Ryle in *The Concept of Mind.*) In addition, there are a number of in-between states of consciousness of which we are aware but may not wish to call sensation or emotion, examples of which are 'interest', 'equanimity', 'curiosity', 'benevolence' and 'malevolence', and which are sometimes referred to as 'dispositions'. Whether or not we can ever be in a 'feeling-less' state is a matter of dispute; I suspect not, only that we are not necessarily *aware* of our feeling-state on all occasions. The feeling-states of which we are aware, and which are usually identified *as* sensations or emotions, are those which are strongly felt so that our attention is drawn to them; they occupy an attention-demanding place in our consciousness, and are frequently regarded as 'disrupting' other activities of consciousness, such as 'thinking' – we cannot 'think straight' because of our toothache or our depression.

Whether or not this is a correct account of the relationship between feeling and reasoning will be discussed later, for the present let us say that feeling (sensation and emotion) is an important component of consciousness, one arising out of our embodied sentient make-up, and one which could be eliminated only by having a completely different composition, one without senses and a nervous system. But another aspect of feeling is *Desiring* – we are conscious of wanting some future state of affairs which, when or if achieved, temporarily abolishes the desire. The unsatisfied desire is experienced as unpleasant so that we direct our efforts to getting rid of it. We are aware of 'wants' and 'needs' and 'yearnings' and 'longings' which range from the most commonplace – the desire for a cup of coffee – to the most complex and intensely experienced – the longing to marry the girl of our dreams. Once again, desiring arises as a result of our having the embodied sentient state we do. At a basic level, because we are *living* beings, it is necessary for us to satisfy our bodily needs in order to survive – we must eat and drink and protect ourselves from various threats to our vulnerable bodies. What is involved in more complex desiring such as wishing to marry the girl of our dreams remains to be seen; perhaps such desiring can be shown to derive from our basic survival needs, perhaps not.

We may now ask how it is that we set about satisfying the desires we experience, what enables us to do this? How is it that we identify what would satisfy our desire? Part of the answer is that we have a 'map' of the world in which we find ourselves which makes it possible for us to recognise what will satisfy, for example, our hunger or thirst, but what is it that makes us seek out what will satisfy our desires? The answer is that we have another activity – *Willing* – which 'pushes' us in the direction of the satisfaction of our desires, and this is something of which we are conscious, we 'feel' it, and when we do not pursue the satisfaction of a desire we are aware of the absence of the required will to do so. Thus, in general, we are aware, as it were, of being 'pulled' by our desires, and 'pushed' by our will. At the same time, we react to this pulling and pushing by means of our *feeling* – it is an indicator of how what we do *affects* us – some of our experience is pleasant, some unpleasant, and we learn, by trial and error, to pursue the pleasant and avoid the unpleasant. If the satisfaction of desire were not pleasant we would not pursue it; if unsatisfied desire were not unpleasant, we would not seek to avoid it by pursuing its satisfaction.

Now, the account given so far holds at a basic level for all living things – in as much as they all pursue the satisfaction of basic needs for *survival* – but many of them do so 'unconsciously', 'intuitively', 'instinctively', by which is meant without 'reflection' on what they are doing. While we say that the plant 'seeks' light, or the amoeba 'pursues' food and 'avoids' poison, we do not mean that they 'know' what they are doing in the sense that they make deliberate decisions to do what they do – they behave automatically or mechanically, we would say. So what is the difference between what all living things do, and the operations of human consciousness? We have seen that we too pursue the fulfilment of the basic needs of living things, so what is the difference between us and 'the rest'?

The difference, as has been pointed out already, is that humans are *self-conscious*, that is, they are aware *that* they are living entities with desires and feelings, and they are also aware, to some extent, *of* the desires and feelings, and of what the possession of desires and feelings *involves* for them. While, in general, they may pursue the pleasant and avoid the unpleasant, they are also capable of doing the opposite on occasion and, usually, in the short term. And this is because humans have the capacity to 'look beyond' the satisfaction of short-term desires, to the satisfaction of long-term ones which may involve putting aside short-term satisfactions. And this is because they have the ability to 'envisage' future possible states of affairs which, temporally, lie a long way beyond the demands of their present context, as I have pointed out in my discussion of imagining and perceiving and remembering.

Thus we can talk about the way in which the experience of human beings is unavoidably affected and structured, one might almost say 'dictated', by their embodied sentient natures. We cannot avoid experiencing desiring and feeling and willing because that is how we as living things 'work', and we cannot avoid being so. Because our cerebral capacity is very much greater than that of non-human animals which means that we spend a great deal of time, and give a great deal of attention to, reasoning and communicating, we tend to ignore or misinterpret the crucial role of feeling and desiring in human experience. Without them there would be *no* experience, or no experience that we would recognise *as* human. Thus, one can say that *all* human experience is *felt* in the sense that it is the experience *of* sentient beings whose contact with their context is *by means* of physical bodies with highly-developed nervous systems which give them the experience they have.

Purposes, Reasons and Causes

Let us now say a little more about how *human* desiring is satisfied. We have already pointed out that in the absence of *self*-consciousness, itself the outcome of larger cerebral capacity than that of non-human animals, one cannot say that desires are satisfied in any more than an intuitive or instinctual way, but in human consciousness the pursuit of the satisfaction of desires may be characterised as *purposive*. What is meant by this is best explained by reference to the distinction between *cause* and *purpose,* or between *causes* and *reasons.* To put the matter simply we may say that causes 'push from behind' while purposes and reasons 'pull from in front'. It is difficult to proceed with the distinction without saying something about what is probably *the* philosophical problem which bedevils almost all philosophical discussion, and that, as I have already mentioned, is *free will* and *determinism.* Again to put the matter simply, this revolves around the question of whether everything that happens does so as a result of some *antecedent* state of affairs which means that an event or state of affairs *must* occur because it is part of an unchangeable pattern or chain of events, or whether it is possible to *intervene* in these apparently unchangeable networks and divert or stop them.

There is no agreement among philosophers on this issue: those who hold the first view are known as Hard Determinists, those who hold the second as Libertarians, while another position known as Compatibilism holds that *some* events and states of affairs are determined but others not. The distinction between causes and reasons is inextricably bound up with this issue because the term 'cause' is usually understood to mean not only that some antecedent state of affairs has brought about the one under consideration, but also that it was *inevitable* that it should be so. If we turn now to our present topic, the satisfaction of desires by humans, should we say that given the nature of the desires, it is inevitable that humans will seek to pursue them in the way they do because they are 'programmed' so to do, ie they have no *choice* in the matter? While we could say this, and some people do, there is another account which claims that we *do* have some 'say' in both how our desires are satisfied, as well as whether they are. We may put it in this way: that because we are *self*-conscious and therefore aware of our desires, and also of the various *possibilities* available to us for satisfying them, or for not doing so, we formulate *purposes* (or goals or aims) which we judge to be the best way of dealing with the demands of our desiring, feeling natures.

On this account, we identify our desire as requiring such-and-such a satisfaction and 'plan ahead' to achieve it. If we were not constantly in a state of unsatisfied desire we would not *do* anything, but this way of putting the matter is perhaps misleading because it suggests that we are constantly racked by agonising gnawings and longings, an unfortunate consequence of the absence of an adequate vocabulary for discussing desiring. Not all desiring is painful, much of it is the motor for our everyday activity, some of which may be enjoyable, or even of little particular significance for us. *All* human activity is purposive in the sense not only that we could not do anything unless we are aware that we are doing it *in order to* bring about some future state of affairs, neither could we explain to ourselves or anyone else *what* we are doing without giving an account of the 'in-order-to' type. Of course we engage in habitual activity without 'realising' what we are doing, but this is the exception. Much of the time we are well aware of what it is we are trying to achieve; even the most humble aim like crossing the room to find a handkerchief, or shutting the window to exclude a draught, is purposive in nature. A way of putting this is to say that our desires are articulated as purposes – we desire some future state of affairs which we *want* to be the case and pursue it *purposefully*. To take one of the present examples, our desire is to blow our nose with a handkerchief and our purpose is to obtain the handkerchief in order to do so. When we have done so, our desire is satisfied, our purpose fulfilled. And the desire has arisen in the first place, presumably, because we dislike having a snuffly nose and wish to change that state of affairs for a preferable one – an unblocked nose.

Certainly the formulation of the purpose involves knowing the location of our handkerchief and that blowing our nose will bring about the required relief, so that some acquaintance with the ways of ordinary human life is necessary, and we shall discuss this at a later stage. So far we have seen that what we do is dictated in the first instance by something we *feel*, in this case a discomfort we wish to be rid of, but we also feel desires as a result of encountering or envisaging an object or state of affairs we would like to possess or take part in, that is, the desire is created by the encounter or envisaging; it did not exist beforehand. While we may already feel hungry and thus seek food to satisfy our hunger, our hunger may also be created by the sight of a delicious confection so that the relations between desires and purposes vary accordingly – sometimes a desire pre-exists the purpose necessary for its fulfilment and there may be a variety of ways of satisfying the desire; sometimes the purpose or endpoint generates the desire, that is, it pre-exists the desire. But in both cases desires are articulated as purposes, and purposes are that towards which desires are directed. We do not regard objects or states of affairs in which we have no interest *as* purposes – what *makes* them 'purposes' is that we desire them and wish to possess them, partake in them, or bring them about. When or if we have done so, we are *satisfied*, and this is something we *feel*, we speak of 'a *sense* of satisfaction' about an accomplished purpose.

Thus desiring is strongly felt, perhaps the most strongly experienced feature of consciousness, and certainly the one which 'keeps us going', the *motor* of all our activity. Without desire we would do nothing, because nothing would attract us or repel us; we would be aware of no 'needs', 'longings', 'yearnings' and 'dissatisfactions'. There would be nothing to draw us towards or push us away from *alternative* states of affairs. How it is that we can be aware of future states of affairs has already been discussed so let us now ask how desiring is related to feeling and willing, because I have claimed that they are closely connected with one another.

The first observation is that what I have said about desiring is very like the sort of things we say about feeling, ie sensation and emotion. What is the difference between them, if there is one? If we *feel* our desires, how do they differ from what are more standardly called our 'feelings'? We cannot say it is because desires are directed towards objects or states of affairs because we say that of feelings too, but we can perhaps say that desires are directed towards *future* (not yet actual) states of affairs, or not yet possessed objects, whereas feelings and emotions are felt *about* both present and future possible objects and states of affairs – they *accompany* our desires, and influence the way in which we pursue their satisfaction, or even whether we pursue them. While, in general, it might seem that we would not *desire* something which does not attract us, something which, for example, we *fear*, it may well be that what we fear is something *en route*, as it were, to the satisfaction of the desire, and which has to be 'lived through' in order to satisfy the primary desire. If we are hungry and have no food in the house we may risk walking through a dark wood, which we fear, in order to obtain food. Thus part of the exercise of satisfying the desire – an attractive future state of affairs – involves experiencing an unpleasant emotion, fear, which we would normally attempt to avoid.

Certainly our fear of the dark wood may be so great that we would rather stay hungry than venture through it; this is as likely as that we would overcome our fear of the wood in order to satisfy our hunger. Thus one might say that sensations and emotions provide 'markers' on the map of our world – they indicate to us how objects and states of affairs do or are likely to *affect* us – we find some attractive, others repellent, yet others puzzling and incomprehensible – and how we are affected influences the way in which we formulate and pursue our purposes (themselves the articulation of desires). The point is that for *human* consciousness, because we have a much greater awareness of the complexity of possible purposes, and of what is involved in pursuing them, we frequently experience tension or conflict both between desires themselves and within the possible means of satisfying them. In this sense, feelings too are motors of what we do – a thicket of prickly bushes may be best avoided in most circumstances but if to go through it is the best way of achieving some desire – to catch a thief, for example – then we may well put up with being horribly scratched in order to do so. To be horribly scratched is unpleasant, but so is losing the family silver to a thief. We may not care about the loss of the silver, and certainly obtain no pleasure from chasing the thief, but we desire to please our family who *will* be upset by the loss; or perhaps we fear our family so much that we desire to avert their ire by attempting to recover their valued property.

Analysis of any reasonably complex situation will yield similar components where it is difficult to disentangle the interrelations between our feelings and our desires. What is clear is that both are *affective*; we constantly adjust our desires relative to our feelings and vice versa, or disregard the one in favour of the other, as I have tried to show with these two examples. *How* our desires are articulated as purposes is in part dependent on our feelings about what is involved in attempting to satisfy the desire; equally, we may 'kill' the desire as a result of reflecting on the likely 'price' to be paid in terms of feeling. All the activities of consciousness interact with one another, so that it is unavoidably artificial to discuss them separately, but it *is* unavoidable. What I am emphatically *not* suggesting is that we are always successful in the juggling act involved: we frequently make mistakes and fail to keep all the balls in the air. All I am trying to do is to tease out what the interrelations are between the activities of consciousness which make our experience what it is, and which enable us to function, at least some of the time. Whether the outcome of the exercise will enable us to 'improve our performance' remains to be seen.

So far we have said something about desiring, feeling and purpose; what can be said about *willing*? I suggested earlier that we are aware of willing, we experience it as that which 'pushes' us towards the satisfaction of our desiring. The question is whether or not it is therefore a part of desiring or something separate which we can 'activate' *in order to* satisfy our desires. There is a difference between 'blind' willing and 'conscious' willing, that non-human animals are subject to the first and human beings are not, or only sometimes. We have seen from the previous piece of discussion that we can sometimes choose *which* pathways we follow to the achievement of our purposes, or rather, we *consider* that we can and do so choose. But can we, 'really', or are we merely having our pathways determined by antecedent states of affairs? Certainly we are aware of deliberating and reflecting, 'choosing' and 'formulating' what seems to be the most efficacious and painless route, and rejecting effortful and painful ones, but is this something which is determined by the strength and nature of the desire so that our pursuit of it is 'inevitable', whatever our own view of the matter may be? Again, there is no conclusive answer to this question. All one can say is that we are *aware* of our deliberations and choices *as* deliberations and choices, ie predicated on the assumption that we *do* have some freedom to choose whether to do X rather than Y and that this, in the view of some philosophers, makes all the difference: the difference between *being* determined and *determining* – between passive and active status *vis-à-vis* one's experience.

So we have a different awareness when we consider that we are initiating an action ourselves from when we consider that we are acting 'against our will'. In the first case we consider that we could have done otherwise; in the second that we had no choice – the two types of experience 'feel different'. In the second case we are aware of resistance from within ourselves to what is occurring; in the first there is no resistance, rather a 'willingness' that whatever it is should occur – we are exercising our will to bring it about because we wish it. A way of putting the matter is to say that in the second case we feel that we are *coerced*, but that we have no sense of coercion in the first case. While this distinction makes sense it still doesn't solve the problem of whether or not the actions in which we do not feel coerced may not themselves be subject to some coercion of which we are not aware, so that in fact we could *not* have done otherwise than we do, and the sense of freedom is an illusion.

There are many accounts of human nature which argue exactly this: that human beings are as subject to forces and determinants beyond their control as any non-human, non-living entity, and that consequently our proud claims to act outside or independent of such determinants are mistaken. There is no solution to this problem, we can only decide to act *as-if* we have the freedom to choose, at least some of the time, because the whole of human existence is predicated on the assumption that we do. The deliberations involved in the formulation and execution of purposes presuppose that there is some *point* in choosing one alternative rather than another. Similarly, as observed above, our interactions with one another presuppose that individuals are *responsible* for what they do or don't do, and this involves assuming that they could have chosen to do otherwise; if they could not there would be no point in *praising or blaming* them for their actions, and we do this all the time.

How does this relate to the notion of *willing*? When we will something we are conscious of 'bringing it about' – we have a recognisably intimate relationship with the act we are engaged with – we feel it is *our* action, we are responsible for it, and that it is directly related to *our* desire articulated as a purpose. Our action is 'directed towards' the fulfilment of the desire/ purpose. It is not that we have randomly moved towards its fulfilment, or even *been* pushed towards it, rather we push *ourselves* towards it. Thus we are able to distinguish between those acts we *voluntarily* undertake, and those which are *in*-voluntary – not of our choosing. And so we could see willing as the means by which we achieve our purposes, and over which we have control. This is different from those actions in which we are involved which do not contribute to the fulfilling of a purpose of ours, and/or occur in spite of our wishes.

There are many occasions of the latter – some people would claim that their whole lives have been of this nature, that either or both their *own* purposes/wishes/desires have not been realised and/or they have been caught up in the actions of others over which they have had no control, and this is undoubtedly correct in many cases.

From what has been said so far we are beginning to arrive at a picture of human individuals as sentient entities which, because of the ability to reflect on themselves and their situation (ie being *self*-conscious), articulate their desires – what they *want* in the way of *future* preferable states of affairs – as purposes or aims or goals, and plan pathways for their fulfilment or achievement or satisfaction. In order to bring about this satisfaction, they *will* or 'push' themselves towards the goal in question, and are conscious that they do so. When the pathways are blocked, individuals are conscious of the obstruction as a resistance to their willing and may either strive to remove it, or else abandon the attempt.

These observations now bring us to the point where we can say something about the role of *feeling* in the feeling-desiring-willing nexus. If we see human beings as fundamentally desiring, feeling entities, sensitive to what they experience, and constantly wanting future states of affairs (desires) which are articulated as purposes, then attempts to achieve these will be sources of pleasure and pain according to whether or not the desires are satisfied, and obstructions will be experienced as painful, and the absence of obstructions as pleasurable. We can now begin to see how feeling fits into this account: at a basic survival level, the possession of senses enables the living entity to negotiate its way around its context, avoiding survival-threatening experiences, and pursuing survival-enhancing ones, not always successfully, of course. Even the simplest living entity can be said to have desires insofar as it is living – it 'wishes' to continue to do so; so that it will seek out nourishment and avoid life-threatening situations: but it will do this 'blindly' because it could not articulate its desires or explain why it pursues nourishment and avoids danger – it just does. When we come to the far more complex experience of *humans* we find the same fundamental underlying structure to what they do, but because they *are* far more complex there is an additional layer, as it were, made up of the operations of self-consciousness, and it is these we have begun to discuss. The simplest living entity is sensitive to stimuli, so are humans; the simplest living entity 'pursues' means towards its survival, so do humans; but the complexities of human consciousness involve humans in *deliberating* and *reflecting* on these activities, and, as it were, providing a commentary on what they are doing.

It is unlikely that the humble woodlouse, finding that it cannot get out of a matchbox, experiences any great suffering although its 'desires' and 'purposes' are being frustrated, and it will constantly 'try' to escape until it perishes for lack of nourishment. The imprisoned human being *will* experience great suffering because they are *aware* that their confinement is blocking their desire to do all sorts of things they *want* to do. They will have a fairly clear idea of this, and they will also be aware that it will be some time before they are likely to be able to satisfy their desires. Thus they will experience suffering which is not fundamentally *physical* (unless for example they are chained up) but it is nonetheless very real and strongly felt. They will experience fear and anger and despair, and these *emotions* are identified and defined in terms of an *appreciation* of the situation in which they find themselves. Similarly, when they are released, or merely hear that they will shortly be released, they will experience joy and relief in the realisation that the obstructions to their desires are soon to be removed. There will almost certainly be physical concomitants to these emotions – weeping with rage or delight, shivering with fear, increased heartbeats, etc – but these are not the emotions themselves.

Thus we can say, in general, that we experience *emotions* as a result of our reflective appreciation of the role we occupy in the context in which we find ourselves, and of the likely significance of it for our *own* experience. It has been suggested that a way of talking about emotions is to say that they have a 'cognitive core', and if by this is meant what I have said above, then that is acceptable, but it is important not to lose the 'felt' nature of emotions, because the 'cognitive' appraisal of the individual's situation does not remove the feeling, rather, it may well intensify it.

Consider a situation in which a person is jealous of their rival for the affections of another. While the cognitive core of this is that the individual has correctly appraised that the other *is* indeed a rival, this realisation does not diminish the strength of their feeling; it is more likely to increase it.

And so we can distinguish between what we might call *primary* and *secondary* desires and emotions. Primary desires and emotions are 'unavoidable' in that they are necessary for the survival of the living entity – any living entity needs to eat, drink, avoid threats and dangers if it is to survive; it is also necessary for it to reproduce to ensure the continuation of the species. *Why* living things have this urge to survive or 'rage to live' is unanswerable; they just do have it, and the imperatives of survival are common to all living things. However, in the case of humans, the matter is complicated by the fact that in addition to the primary desires and emotions necessary for survival (to eat and drink, etc, and to fear predators and/or attack them, ie anger and aggression) we find a whole range of secondary desires and emotions, the outcome of our ability to reflect and deliberate self-consciously on our situations, which exist alongside the primary ones, and which are sometimes in conflict with them so that choices have to be made whether or not to pursue the satisfaction of the primary desire rather than the secondary one. For example, should we put off our desire to drink coffee in order to finish writing a poem?

Painful or uncomfortable interim states of affairs may be a necessary prelude to the satisfaction of a primary desire, but this is a different sense of 'primary' – here we mean that which is apprehended as what we most want. And what we most want may or may not be a primary desire in the first sense. It may be something which is essential for survival, or it may be something which is of supreme importance to us although it is *not* essential for survival – we may desire above anything to finish writing our poem, and are prepared to eschew drinking, eating and sleeping to achieve it. Pangs of hunger and thirst, and weariness, may torment us but we continue with the task. In this case, a secondary desire is 'promoted' to the status of a primary one – we might call it a *principal* desire to distinguish it from primary desires, and call the means to its achievement *subsidiary* desires – and the accompanying emotions are organised in terms of that fact – we are angry if we are interrupted, or fearful that the telephone will ring. Thus we have primary and secondary desires, and principal and subsidiary ones, the first being directly concerned with physical survival, the second with the individual's self-articulated *values* which may be in conflict with the desires of the first category.

This, surely, is the crucial difference between *human* experience and that of all other living things – we have the capacity and the need to *order* or *organise* or *manage* our desires and emotions, making decisions as to what we most want, and putting aside desires which impede the satisfaction of it, and 'noting' and assessing the accompanying emotions in terms of the extent to which they satisfy or fail to satisfy the desire, or fulfil or achieve the purpose which is its articulation. Some aspects of the pursuit of a purpose are enjoyable, others are not – we are angry or frustrated or fearful when our pursuit is obstructed, joyful or delighted when it is not. Furthermore, in addition to the formulation and satisfaction of *our own* desires, we are aware of the desires and emotions of *other* humans and are affected by them in a variety of ways. For example, the purposeful pathways or trajectories of others may come into conflict with our own, or they may coincide; or we may change our own purposes to fall in with those of another or others, and as with our own purposes, the pathways to their achievement will generate a variety of emotions, some pleasant, some unpleasant, but pathways are not abandoned because of their unpleasant aspects if the endpoint is *judged* to be worthwhile, and no alternative means of achieving it is available.

Therefore, while we can say that humans share a number of fundamental features with all other living things – the urge to survive, vulnerability and dangers and threats from the physical world and from one another, sensitivity to stimuli and the capacity to respond to them – they also differ from them as a result of the possession of *self*-consciousness so that one could say that they operate at an *additional* level of experience. This additional level involves the ability to reflect on and deliberate about their experience; to identify and assess various features of their consciousness and organise them in order to satisfy their desires or achieve their purposes. That is, humans have the capacity to *envisage future states of affairs* in terms of which of their desires and purposes are articulated, and to *choose* among possible pathways to their satisfaction. In general, the satisfaction of desires or achievement of purposes is experienced as pleasant, and the obstruction of them as unpleasant or painful, but the pleasure and pain are not only or even primarily *physical* – experienced through the senses – although physical concomitants usually accompany the felt conscious experience we call *emotions.* The pursuit of purposes/satisfaction of desires is brought about by *willing* ie the 'motor' of the activity, and this is, to some extent, under the control of the individual consciousness – we are aware of a difference between those activities we consider we initiate and those which we do not, but which happen *to* us, over which we have no control.

So far we have said something about imagining, perceiving, feeling, desiring and willing, and tried to show how they contribute to human consciousness. However, they only *contribute*; this is not the whole story. Other activities interweave with them to make up human experience as lived, but it is difficult to avoid the artificiality of discussing them separately.

Let us now move on to what many consider to be the most important human activity or capacity – *reasoning*.

Reasoning and Judging

In much of the history of Western philosophy, up to and including analytic philosophy in the twentieth century and beyond, reasoning has been very thoroughly explored, sometimes to the downgrading if not exclusion of other activities of consciousness. This has sometimes led to the claim that humans are, par excellence, *reasoning* animals, and this defines them, and distinguishes them from other (supposedly lesser) living entities.

For the purposes of this book, which stresses the *equal* centrality of imagining and desiring among the activities of consciousness, I shall outline only the two main types of reasoning – the *theoretical* and the *practical,* both very carefully explored by eg Aristotle and Kant, among others.

Kant's discussions are of dizzying complexity (later modified and simplified by Schopenhauer) but what emerges is this:

Theoretical reasoning aims to describe and explain the world of our experience in terms of the formulation of concepts, types or classes of entities, and the causal relations between them, in order to enable us to *understand* (as far as possible) the world, and to give an account of it as well as predict future states of affairs in the light of such causal relations.

Practical reasoning, on the other hand, aims to investigate, not what *is* the case (the task of theoretical reasoning) but what we *should* do in order to find our way about the context in which we find ourselves, and to formulate *rules* in order to do so. These rules constitute what is usually called *morality,* and the philosophical discussion of them, *Ethics.*

We have already seen that, because of our ability to envisage the possible future, we *order* our desires in the light of such envisaging, putting aside short-term desires in order to achieve the satisfaction of long-term ones. We *value* the latter over the former. Rather roughly formulated 'rules of conduct' aid (or impede) this, and, in any case, because they are always changing, we quickly run out of rules, or descend into an infinite regress of formulating rules for the application of rules! In which case, we have no option but recourse to what might be called *judging* or, to put it trivially, to 'hoping for the best', (Mother Wit, as Kant rather charmingly puts it), fingers crossed behind our backs. But this, surely, *is* how we proceed. We can never formulate an accurate and reliable anticipation of the future, because it has not happened yet. A disaster of global proportions makes us run around like headless chickens, former moral guidance in need of modification. Luckily, however, the ceaseless creativity of consciousness gives us some hope that solutions might be found, and a new, amended set of rules formulated. It is a mistake to think that *any* set of rules is 'written in stone', unchanged and unchangeable, however great our longing for certainty and fixity.

How humans *do* interact with one another (at present) will be explored in Part Two, and some suggestions will be made as to how they *might* interact more fruitfully.

Communicating

As with reasoning, the details of language formation and use have been very thoroughly explored – by Linguistics, Philosophy of Language, Philology, Psychology, Sociology, Ethology *et al.*

It is by means of language, however defined, that we communicate with one another, and, arguably with non-human animals, or, even more arguably, with plants and the natural world. Gardeners and ramblers sometimes claim that they 'talk to plants/nature', and have some sort of response.

For our purposes, *communicating* is one more important activity of consciousness which interweaves incessantly with all the others. Not to want to, try to or be able to is viewed with some suspicion nowadays and is sometimes over-readily 'diagnosed' as a worrying medical 'condition' called *Autism*, which should be identified and 'treated'. If humans are indeed reasoning animals, they are also *sociable* animals, because, the argument goes, so much of worth in human experience comes from their interaction with one another.

While this may be so in *some* cases, where inability to communicate is considered to be positively disabling, we must not apply the term 'autism' too loosely or too hastily. What of the 'natural' recluses who 'prefer their own company'? What of those, usually religious, who take a vow of silence in the belief that this encourages and enables communion with the

Transcendent? Should such people be 'brought into line' and urged to be 'more sociable'?

Some people claim to need quite long periods of peace and quiet in order to have any chance of thoughts and ideas of any quality, and many writers, artists, composers and academics would agree with them. However, there are exceptional and admirable people who do produce high-quality work alongside eg cooking a meal, doing the laundry or/and pacifying squabbling small children, or even running a business or pursuing a professional career eg doctors and lawyers. The distinguished Orientalist and Sinologist Arthur Waley claimed that he could work unruffled on his translations in the midst of air-raids in London during World War Two!

Surely, then, those who choose an *unsocial* life should be left to do so. Nowadays, 'talking to one another' is viewed as a panacea for all manner of ills, evidenced by the proliferation of 'talking cures' which may indeed have their place, but much which was formerly regarded as private is now made public.

Attempting to communicate with others does contribute to *self*-understanding as well as *other*-understanding, as we shall see in Chapters Two and Four, but frequently such attempts result in little more than mindless chatter, and what may pass for spirited debate may be only 'full of sound and fury, signifying nothing' (Shakespeare, *Macbeth*), and while this may oil the wheels of social intercourse, it does little more than that. Social media, also, do little more than this, as often as not, and may be harmless, but also have their dark sides: cyberbullying being an example of this.

Enormous problems are involved in communicating, not least the problem of how a *speaker* tries to 'say what they mean' and the hearer to understand this without distortion and misunderstanding: as has been thoroughly discussed endlessly by linguists, philosophers of language and psychologists. This may include the vexed issue of body-language, now regarded as of more importance than often hitherto.

The difficulties are great enough when speakers and hearers speak the *same* languages; they are compounded when *different* languages are involved, where definitions and connotations are so varied, as any translator will confirm. Much has been written on this theme, which I shall not pursue, but rather concentrate first on the subject of the *self*.

2

INDIVIDUATION AND ITS IMPLICATIONS

IT CANNOT BE STRESSED TOO MUCH that consciousness occurs in *individuated* sensate, embodied entities: such entities normally move about, *feel* pleasure and pain, and are aware of themselves *as* both separate from but also connected to other such entities. That is, they are aware of themselves as unique individuals.

1) IDENTIFICATION OF THE SELF

With this in mind, let us consider how this separateness is experienced by discussing both the identification and the organization of the self.

It has taken some time throughout human history for the notion of *individuation* to emerge. Formerly, the *exigencies* of survival (providing basic needs and repelling threats) meant that human beings were obliged to remain in groups, and to formulate *collective* rules in order to stay alive.

The slow separation of an individuated self, separate from the group or collective, has been very well charted by Charles Taylor in *Sources of the Self.*

Personal Identity

For philosophers, personal identity is a *problem,* for non-philosophers it is not, or only occasionally – at any rate, until the recent widespread interest in 'identity', both personal and social (as indicated by such TV programs as *Who Do You Think You Are?*). We all have a very strong basic, fundamental sense of our own identity in that we are convinced we a) are separate from other individuals and b) know *who* we are for most practical purposes, ie can give some account of what qualities we possess which contribute to distinguishing ourselves from others, and to describing ourselves to ourselves and to others, eg 'I am male, white, Scottish, twenty-six years old, and an accountant by profession'. We could go into more detail, if required, spelling out our parentage, education, hobbies etc. Normally, at no point do we wonder if we exist at all, whether we might be someone else, or how peculiar it is to be a human individual in the first place rather than an ant or a tree, although these are the sort of questions bright children begin to ask, and continue to ask if they have a philosophical cast of mind.

However, there are some circumstances in which even non-philosophers are forced to consider some version of this type of question – when, for example, mental or physical illness changes a person's personality so that others say that they no longer recognise them as 'the same person'. Similarly, reflections on death may cause people to wonder whether some form of existence might persist when the body decays, and if it does, *how* it could. What sort of existence could it be? Topically, many people are now wondering how to make sense of human cloning in which hitherto unique individuals are no longer unique, as there is another (or several others) of them. What does this mean for our sense of our own identity? It is certainly unsettling to consider that there might be another one of us in existence at the same time as us though in a different place.

It is from questioning of this sort that the philosophical problem of personal identity arises and is developed, sometimes to bizarre lengths, generating thought experiments of vertiginous complexity, some of which may provide illumination and some not. I shall not attempt to summarise the extensive philosophical discussions of the topic, although it is now fashionable to question one's 'identity' in terms of ethnic origins, gender etc; rather I shall select from it those issues which I consider relevant to my main concerns.

The first issue concerns what it is that makes us consider that we are the *same* person although our spatio-temporal position constantly changes. Is there *something* that persists throughout these changes? A way of putting it is to ask if there is some sort of 'glue' which holds together all the disparate features which make up our identity. Various answers have been given, ranging from the idea of an immortal soul or 'essence', to our physical bodies, or our physical bodies plus a set of associated psychological characteristics, or a set of memories of past experiences which we recognise as uniquely *ours*. There is no agreement among philosophers as to which of these provides a correct answer, and I have no new contribution to make to the discussion. I prefer to view personal identity as a fragile composite of all of these; fragile because our sense of our own identity is easily lost or disrupted, a composite because we appeal to all these features when we attempt to characterise ourselves to ourselves, or to others.

The most persistent-seeming feature is probably our physical body, the envelope in which we carry on our lives. In spite of the fact that it changes over time, we continue to recognise it as *ours*. When we look in the mirror we see the same face day after day, give or take a few wrinkles, bags under the eyes or grey hairs. After a serious illness we may say that we do not recognise ourselves but this does not mean that we seriously consider that we have become another person, only that the same person has changed a great deal. Certainly if we had the experience of Franz Kafka's (human) character who wakes up to find he is a cockroach (ie has a cockroach's *body*) in the story 'The Metamorphosis', we would have reason to be extremely alarmed. We literally would not know what to think, leaving aside all the problems of whether or not we would have a cockroach's brain and therefore a cockroach's 'thoughts'. Fantasy aside, in spite of considerable changes our bodies persist as recognisably 'ours' throughout our lives, and while we may regret the changes, there is no radical questioning of whether or not it is 'our' body rather then somebody else's. (We might mention here transsexual and transgender individuals, defined in relation to a gender identity either not consistent with or not confined by their biologically assigned sex.)

Doubts about 'who we are', then, must arise from some other quarter, from our psychological characteristics and/or our memories. We experience 'psychological characteristics' as feelings, tastes, capacities and vulnerabilities, values. We like certain things and dislike others; we are attracted to some things and repelled by others; we fear some things and are irritated by others; we can do some things and are no good at others; we approve of some things and disapprove of others. These feelings, tastes etc cash out in psychological descriptions of our 'personalities' along the lines of 'nervous', 'confident', 'bad-tempered, 'equable', 'good at games', 'ham-fisted', 'tolerant', 'censorious' and so on, so that any individual will be made up of a patchwork of such characteristics, ones which may be modified over time but usually remain relatively stable features of their 'make-up'. As a result of eg education or traumatic experience they may be dramatically modified, some features virtually disappearing, others manifesting themselves apparently for the first time. Even in these cases, we do not say, except colloquially, that the individual has become 'another person', only that the *same* person has changed dramatically. Presumably this is because, however great the psychological changes, their *body* remains recognisable as 'theirs', and they continue to stand in the same relations to others as they did before the changes, that is, they will still be taken to be the same person by their familes, their colleagues, neighbours etc, although a greatly changed person. Certainly, as a result of such dramatic changes, these relations may change – their families reject them, they lose their job, the neighbours no longer speak to them, but the conviction will remain that 'fundamentally' they are the *same* person.

But what about those occasions on which the individual *themselves* no longer feel that they are the same person? In the case of advanced insanity some individuals become convinced that they *are* Jesus Christ or Napoleon; in less serious cases individuals may be merely in a state of great confusion about 'who they are' in the sense that they can neither give an account of themselves to themselves, or to others, and others are unable to characterise *them* because of these incomprehensible accounts. Nonetheless, a recognisably 'same' body persists even though what 'inhabits' it is very confused. This applies equally to those who have lost their memories – *others* recognise them as the same person, although they do not recognise themselves, ie cannot give any account of themselves *to* others. Thus it seems that a persistent recognisable physical body is the fundamental criterion of personal identity: individuals primarily are entities occupying a unique spatio-temporal location. They are unique because no other entity is precisely the same as them – even an identical twin or a clone occupies a different spatio-temporal location.

At this point it might be useful to make a distinction between asking *what* one is and asking *who* one is, because each question highlights different issues and generates different answers. I suggest that to ask *what* one is will generate an answer along the lines sketched out above – human individuals are unique composites of a spatio-temporally distinct physical body plus a series of memories pertaining to it plus a set of psychological characteristics. All these features are subject to change over time so that Ii at Ti will not be identical with Iii at Tii, although there will be enough persistent similarity between them for them and for others to consider them the *same* person *under normal circumstances.*

If we now address ourselves to the question of *who* one is, we come closer to the central concerns of this book, because in my view this is where we confront the issues of whether or not an individual is the *source* of their purposive actions, and whether or not they can be held *responsible* for those actions. Thus we meet the matter of *autonomy* and *agency* head-on, and these will be discussed further in the next section. Only if one has a clear idea of *who* one is in the sense of understanding one's own nature, one's preferences, tastes, capacities and vulnerabilities, is one in a position either to formulate intentions or initiate actions in any meaningful way. Only if one has such meaningful intentions and actions can one take responsibility for or be held responsible for their consequences. And such responsibility presupposes at least a compatibilist position ie one in which one could have done otherwise had one so chosen.

Assuming this starting point, how is self-understanding to be acquired? What would count as an answer to the 'Who am I?' question in this sense? We have already mentioned the matter of psychological characteristics: how are these identified? Surely by a combination of self-observation and other-observation. We ask ourselves what we think about or feel about some state of affairs; we ask others (or are told unasked!) how we *appear* to think and feel about the state of affairs. From reflection on these two processes we formulate a tentative view of what sort of person we are. I say 'tentative' because one is constantly revising and updating, therefore re-creating, one's view of oneself in the light of new experience. The difficulty is that such understanding is *always* mediated or filtered or refracted *by the views of others*, others who do not have access to one's 'insider' acquaintance with one's own experience; but at the same time, that insider acquaintance is far from clear to oneself on many occasions – how often do we say 'I don't know what I think about that', or 'I don't know how I feel about that' – and we look to others to clarify the matter for us, although when they do so we may not agree with them. But it is only through such conversational exchanges that we stand any chance of achieving self-understanding, as I shall discuss in more detail later on (see Chapter Four). It is very common for individuals to say or do one thing and be thought by others to have said or done something quite different. And even if it is agreed by both parties that an individual is, for example, irascible, there may be considerable disagreement as to the occasions on which the expression of irascibility is *justified.* This in turn can lead to a lengthy analysis of the context in which the expression has occurred, thus the *identification* of psychological characteristics is only a beginning: subsequent stages could involve discussion of whether or not the possession of such a characteristic is to be admired or abhorred; of whether or not one could decide that *per se*, without knowledge of the context, because eg what is regarded as courage on one occasion is thought to be recklessness on another.

The main point is that since we do not usually have all the time in the world to discuss these matters, we work with very approximate and frequently grossly inaccurate notions of both ourselves and others which enable us to get by but not much more.

It may be asked why it *matters* to have anything more than these approximations and the answer is that it is a matter of justice, fairness and (dare I use the word?) truth, however defined, to try to describe ourselves and others as accurately as possible since a great deal depends on it, as I shall try to show. And this is *not* just a matter of concern to philosophers, the whole of human existence is shot through with the demand that we shall try to be as accurate as we can in all we say and do – that we should say what we mean and not lie; that we should describe and explain matters as accurately as we can rather than misrepresent or calumniate; that we should treat others as fairly and justly as we can if we are to expect them to treat us in the same way. And one crucial component of this way of proceeding is that we should try to be as clear as possible about ourselves and 'what we stand for', and hope to be equally clear about at least some others – those with whom we come into significant contact – because only in these circumstances is any meaningful interaction possible. Furthermore, such self-understanding is the basis for any intelligible notion of *self-creation*, as Jonathan Glover calls it in *I: The Philosophy and Psychology of Personal Identity*. There are two issues which complicate the search for self-understanding: Temperament, and Self-deception and Self-esteem. Let us turn to these.

Temperament

The colloquial understanding of this term is something along the lines of 'the sort of person one is', where the features considered relevant are *persistent* 'character traits' such as 'equable', 'trustworthy', 'unreliable', 'hot-tempered', 'eccentric' etc. In such terms we summarise others, and they summarise us. We apply these descriptive terms as a result of long-term observation of others' behaviour, finding that people tend to exhibit similar responses to experience which can be classified in terms of the examples above. An equable person will rarely become angry however great the provocation; an unreliable one will constantly fail to keep appointments or do what they have undertaken to do. In the light of these persistent traits we organise our responses to others, trying to avoid irritating a hot-tempered person, and deciding to make no further arrangements with an unreliable one. But of course the matter is far more complex than this because the relations in which we stand to the other may cause us to override the standard responses – we may tolerate an eccentric person because we love them, or continue to try to trust the unreliable one because we work with them and have no alternative but to do so.

The important question for our purposes is whether or not 'temperament is destiny' (referring back to the Presocratic philosopher Heraclitus), that is, do people have the temperaments they do inevitably, or can they be changed, modified, revised? The debate as to whether or not temperament is a *genetic* inheritance, on a par with blue eyes and black hair, is inconclusive, but while it is not as straightforward as eye and hair colour, there is a good deal of evidence to suggest that people's *basic* temperaments are inherited. The nervous person will continue to be nervous, the bouncy extrovert will continue to bounce, but within these very wide categories there is lots of room for manoeuvre, as anyone familiar with upbringing and education will confirm. If this were not so there would be little point in trying to educate people, because education should do far more than fill people's heads with information: it also *changes* them, sometimes radically, by teaching them 'strategies' for dealing with their own temperamental endowment. Nervous people may learn to overcome their shyness and diffidence, confident ones to moderate their tendency to dominate. All of these things happen all the time, irrespective of philosophical discussion of free will and determinism, because it is of the very nature of human experience for individuals to *affect* one another by praise and blame, encouragement and discouragement, kindness and cruelty. They have been doing this since time began, so to speak, and will continue to do it whatever philosophers may say, although theoretical discussions to the effect that individuals *cannot* be held responsible for what they do because they just are the people they are do impinge on everyday life and influence the way we treat one another.

But such thinking has both advantages and disadvantages. An advantage may be that we are more *tolerant* of others, based on some muddled idea that they cannot help what they do, or being the sort of people they are. As a result of this way of thinking *punishment* has become less harsh and brutal (in *some* parts of the world) but this occurs at the same time as continuing to try to educate them, ie *change* them, which must be based on the assumption that they *can* help what they do and do not *have* to be the people they are – they are capable of *choosing* to do otherwise. Can one hold *both* of these views at the same time without contradiction? I think not. Either individuals *are* capable of changing, or they are not. Obviously they do change as a result of others' treatment of them, in many cases at least, so the question is, can they change *themselves* as a matter of their own choice (because they see the point of doing so)? I suggest that not only are individuals capable of changing themselves if they see the point of doing so, but also that they can only do so meaningfully as a result of clarifying for themselves *what* it is that they want to change – ie that they attempt to achieve self-understanding.

We have already seen that there is often a mismatch between how individuals perceive themselves, and how others perceive them, and that there is no quick and easy way of establishing an accurate picture of 'what someone is like', no scientific test which establishes what a person's nature 'really is', like Tristram Shandy's Momus's glass in the human breast enabling us to gaze into people:

> Had the said glass been set up, nothing more would have been wanting, in order to have taken a man's character, but to have taken a chair and gone softly, as you would to a dioptrical beehive, and looked in.
> – Laurence Sterne, *The Life and Opinions of Tristram Shandy, Gentleman*, ed Graham Petrie, Penguin, 1979, p96

Unfortunately, or perhaps fortunately, such a thing is not possible, so that we are left with the eternally uphill task of trying to obtain as accurate a view as possible of human individuals' 'natures', our own included, a view which can never be complete, not only because of the difficulty just discussed, but also because individuals are constantly *re-creating* themselves in the light of new experience. (However, there are some individuals who resist change and re-creation, hanging on grimly to 'tried and tested' attitudes and views … and prejudices.)

My interim conclusions about temperament, then, are that while we may be genetically endowed with certain *very general* character traits, or dispositions, these are normally susceptible to considerable direction and modification as a result of the efforts of both others and ourselves. If this were not so, there would be no point in education, in human interaction, in anything which *affects* human individuals, because to be affected is to be changed, like it or not. We are constantly changed by our non-human environment (hot weather cheers some of us up; drought makes us anxious), and while these may be short-term responses, they do not have to be. Similarly, our interaction with others changes us, and encourages us to change ourselves in the light of praise and blame etc.

Since no individual, or even group of individuals, is omniscient, we all need some form of *education*; we learn from others, and should and must do so.

In the case of children, who have little or no experience of 'life', some sort of *guidance* is surely imperative, and many different types of education have been suggested or even implemented, in some cases very much to the detriment of 'the taught'.

Could there be some middle way between the Scylla of the harsh practices of eg the former British Public School system (unfortunately mirrored and adopted in other schools), as depicted in Thomas Hughes' novel *Tom Brown's School Days*, or the Charybdis of the wilder excesses of some notions of 'progressive' education in which abdication of any sort of guidance is justified in order not to stunt the 'natural' growth and development of the child?

Self-deception and self-esteem

There are two further impediments in the way of achieving self-understanding. These are self-deception and self-esteem, and the two are inextricably intertwined with one another. Even the most unreflective person is aware that they are the object of others' attention, and that they are placed under some very general description such as 'a nice chap', 'an awkward so-and-so', 'a nasty piece of work', or 'delightful company'. Sometimes one is happy to be perceived in this way, sometimes not.

But quite frequently one's self-image, as it is sometimes called, is wildly at variance with what others *do* actually think of one. Our social relations are so complex that gaining any accurate view of what people think of one another is complicated by a whole network of social mores such as tact, politeness, diplomacy, respect etc, quite apart from the more serious difficulties of trying to work out what one *does* think of another independently of these. People's personalities are fluid, elusive, constantly changing or being re-created, hidden from view much of the time so that we are obliged to resort to the crude approximations mentioned above which do little more than give us a 'working knowledge' of them. In nineteenth century novels characters spend an inordinate amount of time trying to describe and explain one another's personalities, and frequently getting it wrong, as subsequent events demonstrate: consider Jane Austen's seemingly charming young men who turn out to be 'absolute bounders', eg as in *Pride and Prejudice.*

A quite common strategy employed to boost self-esteem is for people to claim to find (invent?) aristocratic *ancestors*, thus giving the impression that *they* are more 'highly-born' than their present humble circumstances would suggest. (See Thomas Hardy's novel *Tess of the d'Urbervilles*.)

Human beings have a very highly-developed capacity to present themselves as other than they are, so that they are capable of deceiving most of the people most of the time. The question of interest to us here is why this capacity *is* so highly-developed.

We have already discussed the first part of an answer by pointing out that individuals themselves are frequently confused as to who they are, in the sense that they do not understand themselves; they do not know what their views are about a whole range of issues; they do not know what they are capable of or how to go about achieving aims which attract them or avoiding situations which they dislike or fear. Little wonder that others find them puzzling, difficult to 'pin down' under any precise description even if they should want to find one. Nevertheless, everyone is obliged to 'keep going', to interact with others, to make decisions and to act on them, and to take responsibility for them, again and again, day in and day out, year in and year out, whether or not they feel capable of doing so. Most of us don't feel capable of coping with what is demanded of us by human existence, because we are aware that it is full of pitfalls and obstacles: so that it is unsurprising that we develop strategies for minimising the concomitant risks. One of these is self-deception, by which we convince ourselves that we are more competent than we are, that we are the sort of person who *can* deal with life's difficulties. We downgrade or ignore our vulnerabilities, and upgrade our capacities, presenting ourselves to others *as* the sort of person we would *like to be*. If this is successful, seeing ourselves reflected in their eyes, as it were, reinforces our conviction that we 'really are' that sort of person. An extreme version, or variation, of this is represented by Patricia Highsmith's character Tom Ripley; in the film version of her novel *The Talented Mr Ripley* (dir Anthony Minghella), Ripley tellingly says that for him it's better to be a false somebody than a real nobody.

This confidence is sometimes dented when others tell us 'home truths', ie describe us in ways we do not like, and we respond to this either by accepting what they say and amending our personalities/behaviour or (more often, perhaps) by objecting to what they say and insisting that our own picture of ourselves is the correct one. In all these cases, what is at issue is our *self-esteem*, a fragile commodity, easily destroyed, sometimes permanently. The writer who receives a damning and insulting review, the teacher who is publicly denounced as incompetent, the doctor who is sued for negligence, the individual who is told by a supposed close friend that they have never really liked them, all these can suffer near-mortal blows to their self-esteem – to their sense of themselves as worthwhile individuals, deserving respect. And the other side of the coin, the *boost* to self-esteem, is equally important because the individual is encouraged to see themselves in a more favourable light than hitherto – the unexpected praise or 'vote of confidence', even the reinforcement of already-existing support from another, can do a great deal to strengthen the cement of an individual's self-image.

A further complication of trying to ascertain who one is, as well as who one *should* be, is that of *evaluation*. Since every disposition carries the potential for evil, as Mr Darcy observes in Jane Austen's *Pride and Prejudice*, and *mutatis mutandis*, the potential for good, one cannot just go through a list of dispositions, even if one has managed to define them with some precision – a difficult enough task, ticking off some as 'good' and others as 'bad'. We have already seen that good-seeming dispositions can become bad-seeming under another description, eg brave/reckless or equable/lazy, and that ascertaining quite what *is* one's view of one's own and others' actions is taxing in the extreme because it is dependent on a fairly detailed understanding of the *context* in which the disposition manifests itself, where this must include some idea of what the individuals themselves considered they were doing. We do the right things for the wrong reasons and the wrong things for the right reasons, so that it is not possible merely to look at the act distinct from what 'motivated' it. We may receive some credit for having a 'well-meant' reason even though the outcome is disastrous; we may be censured for a happy outcome of malign intentions, if these are known. This point is much rehearsed in discussions of Utilitarianism but is equally relevant here. There is always room for error and correction, and this is what we do all the time when we attempt to describe, analyse, criticise and evaluate what human beings do, although perhaps only philosophers would describe it in this way. For most of us converse and gossip and criticise and speculate about one another because we want to understand what makes people 'tick', if only so that we have some idea of how to 'deal with' them: we learn to avoid the 'nasty piece of work', and to seek out the kind-hearted and trustworthy, for example. And sometimes we find that the 'nasty piece of work' has 'a heart of gold', and that the 'trustworthy' person is capable of the utmost treachery. Thus we constantly adjust and revise our views of others (and of ourselves) in the light of new experience.

The main philosophical point underlying this piece of discussion is that determining *who* a person is, is an ineluctably *interactive* process. There is no neutral person-free description which can be determined by some equivalent of Tristram Shandy's Momus's-glass. We have no alternative but to look to ourselves *and* to others in order to try to establish *some* notion of who we are in terms of persistent features of our 'make-up', which are themselves ascertained as a result of looking at how we behave, at what others say of us, at what we say of ourselves, at how others respond to us. And *all* of these are fraught with the difficulties I have tried to spell out. We deceive ourselves and we deceive others, sometimes wittingly, sometimes unwittingly, because:

> We like to be well thought of by others
> So that we may think well of ourselves.
>
> – T.S. Eliot, 'The Family Reunion',
> *The Complete Poems and Plays*, Faber, 1969, p302

And we need to think well of ourselves in order to 'keep going', and possibly so that we may be thought well of by others. The former at least is a psychological *fact* and a philosophical *truth* – a psychological fact because there is ample empirical evidence to show that those who do not think well of themselves cannot function, or only *mal*function (involving breakdowns, criminality etc); a philosophical truth about human nature in as much as praise and blame, encouragement and discouragement, are the very bread and butter of moral reasoning – we can only *understand* human nature in terms of what motivates or causes humans to be the way they are.

Philosophers have not *invented* the view that humans are purposive, feeling, communicating etc entities; all they do is try to give a systematic account of human nature on the basis of the features it *already* exhibits.

We shall explore this further in Part Two.

Alterity

The term 'Alterity' (or 'radical heterogeneity') draws attention to how the individual's *separateness* from other entities, especially other humans, is experienced. The best way of characterising it in the first instance is as *loneliness* or *isolation*. We have seen that the urge 'to belong' is very strong in humans, but that this occurs alongside the urge to 'individuate', to be 'different', and creates a tension if not a conflict, emphasising, as it does, both the similarities with and differences from others. For Emmanuel Levinas, whose work I do not propose to discuss in detail, a given of human experience is our awareness of the absolute inalienable *otherness* of the other (all other humans), and from this he derives a detailed metaphysics and ethics, some aspects of which I adapt in my analysis, most especially the notions of 'the face-to-face' and 'conversation' (see Chapter Three). (Although I have taken the term 'alterity' from Levinas' *Totality and Infinity*, my *use* of the term differs in certain respects from his. In fact, my position is possibly closer to Martin Buber's in his account of what he calls 'I-Thou' relations in his book *I and Thou*; I prefer Levinas' terminology, however.) At present I am concerned only with the individual's own experience. The awareness of the otherness of the other encourages one to disguise this realisation by attempting to unify with the other on the basis of ways in which one *resembles* them (colour of skin, same language, family relationships, contiguity of territory etc), because this provides some *comfort* by diminishing one's sense of loneliness. However, this is likely to come into conflict with what may only be an emergent awareness that one is different from others, not only in physical and psychological characteristics but also in goals and purposes, so that others can be regarded as impediments or obstructions of one's desires because *their* desires and purposes are not *one's* own, although they may resemble them and even on occasion be identical with one's own.

Consequently individuals are aware of themselves as 'beleaguered' by others; there is a 'struggle' for existence even at the most basic level of the need for food and shelter. While communal strategies may exist which make the struggle at this basic level of existence less stark and urgent, once these basic desires are satisfied, *new* desires present themselves because this is of the nature of human consciousness, and these will require the formulation of new purposes. Certainly there can be static societies or groups where new purposes have little chance of formulation, but that is because they are artificially suppressed; human history contains ample examples of apparently static societies changing *sooner or later* into dynamic ones. On the individual level we find the same inevitability of change – difference of tastes, beliefs, and practices, considerable or subtle, are expressed whenever there is the slightest opportunity of doing so. At the same time, and this is the tension, the expression of such differences may be actively discouraged, not only in others but also by individuals themselves, because the urge to 'belong' triumphs over the urge to 'be different': the former is easier, the latter requires 'decision and courage', and is subject to all the difficulties already discussed (uncertainty as to who one is, what one desires etc), so that, ironically, the awareness of alterity reinforces the urge to ignore it, emphasising similarities and suppressing difference.

If this is so, and is a 'natural' response to the problems of individuation, why not continue in this way, especially as stressing similarities may encourage a 'humane' stance towards others, as it undoubtedly can do? The answer is, surely, that to take this one-sided approach is to fly in the face of the essence of human consciousness, the *uniqueness* of human individuals. And to do so produces an ineliminable sense of dis-satisfaction, of 'not-rightness'.

We have seen that enabling individuals to express their unique individuality is no guarantee of success, and carries heavy penalties: existing in the thin air of independence can *increase* rather than *decrease* the individual's sense of loneliness because the responsibility for 'getting it wrong' lies squarely with the individual and is far more uncomfortable to endure than being able to blame someone else for one's failure.

A possibly useful metaphor, borrowed from Physics, might be to say that the urge to individuate is *centrifugal*, while the urge to belong (with others) is *centripetal*. And these two tensions operate all the time within human consciousness.

Is there any way, then, of resolving this dilemma, or is there only the stark choice between the pros and cons of belonging or the pros and cons of individuating? I suggest that the concomitant loneliness and isolation of individuating may not be so acute in a *climate* in which there is *respect for alterity*, ie where it is generally accepted that individuals' differences from one another are as authentic as their similarities. In some ways this suggestion resembles Kant's 'Kingdom of Ends' (in *Groundwork of the Metaphysics of Morals*) but overcomes some of its difficulties. For Kant, The Kingdom of Ends is a community of *autonomous* individuals governed by Reason, but the difficulty with it is that Kant has too much confidence in the *uniformity* of the dictates of Reason. While the replacement of the categorical imperative with respect for alterity may not solve all the problems of Kant's view, its vehicle, *conversation*, being more 'open', 'warm' and immediate than Kant's austere and chilly scenario, may diminish them. One must not underestimate the effect of *hostility and contempt* on human individuals – the most powerful force for the suppression of individual differences – and any proposal which offers a context in which individuals can explore their uniqueness without the threat of being 'put down' is the only one likely to encourage human flourishing.

These matters will be explored more fully in Part Two.

(2) ORGANISATION OF THE SELF

Autonomy, Agents and Patients, Authority

It is now the occasion to think about *how* individual selves can and do express themselves; and how they conduct themselves in the course of their lives. What *pressures* do they experience; what *opportunities* are available to them?

The discussion of the previous section has shown that trying to identify *who* one is, or who anyone is, is problematical in the extreme if what one is seeking is a reliable account which not only describes the person but also enables us to predict with *some* certainty what they are likely to do, or how they might act in the future. Such certainty is very difficult to achieve;

there is ample opportunity for error and no reliable means for correcting such errors apart from endless ongoing *interactive* questioning, revision and amendment as long as the person continues to live and breathe, because it is of the essence of human individuals constantly to change and be changed.

Thus, attempting to understand 'what makes people tick' would appear to be an impossible task, one we would abandon were it not for the fact that we are incessantly obliged to have some sort of working understanding of ourselves and others in order to exist at all in any meaningful way. Human existence would not make any *sense* if it were not based on a whole range of assumptions, usually lying just below the surface of consciousness, about what people are, and what we can expect of them. If we did not do this but merely treated humans as mechanisms we would no longer recognise our experience *as* human. And so, difficult as it is, we must go on trying to understand, and another way of doing this which may yield some insights is to look at how humans perceive and organise themselves *vis-à-vis* one another.

One way of dealing with this so as to minimise the problem is by going along with the purposes of others, relinquishing our own goals or even never having any in the first place. Most of us have learned to do this *some* of the time; it is part of the process of socialisation, but unless we are to become complete will-less zombies, it is not possible to do it all of the time. Our own purposes, dimly articulated as they may be, are driven underground where they fester and fume, causing untold damage according to some psychiatric/psychological thinking. Nonetheless we can see the appeal of the notion of social harmony, and tailor our goals and aspirations to cause minimum disruption in many cases. Unfortunately this leaves the way clear for unscrupulous individuals, unworried by such fine feelings, to pursue *their* purposes unopposed. Every *agent* needs one (or many) *patients.*

But is this inevitable? I would like to think that individuals are not cast in the roles of life-long agents or life-long patients; rather that each of us is sometimes the one and sometimes the other, but that it is within our power to *choose* which it should be. Kant's rousing battle-cry in *What is Enlightenment?*, exhorting the individual to use their *own* understanding (quoted later in this book), of course exaggerates because much of the time we do need to listen to and follow the advice of others. There is no harm in this – nobody is all-wise – but unless individuals are *actively* trying to clarify their own views and purposes, they will have nothing against which to measure such advice, no means of knowing when it is good advice, and when bad, except to wait for the outcome of following it, by which time matters may be irrevocable.

An analysis of three notions may help us to clarify what is at issue here, and these are Autonomy, Agents and Patients, and Authority.

Autonomy

Prima facie it may seem that individuals who themselves choose how to act, and are willing to take responsibility for what they do, are autonomous, that is, they 'rule themselves' rather than being ruled by others or by forces over which they have no control. Other terms which are largely synonymous with 'autonomy' are 'self-determination' and 'authenticity'; in each case what is central is to rule the self, to determine the self, to be the 'author' of oneself, so that individuals apprehend themselves as centre-stage while other individuals are part of the context in which they operate, although these other individuals may or may not be considered to be equally unique autonomous selves. The autonomous condition has not always been considered important or worthwhile: social cohesion in which individual desires and purposes were subsumed under and often identical with those of a group or society was formerly of far more significance. The emergence of autonomy as a prime value is a complex matter but one can say, in general, that individuals increasingly developed a sense of their own uniqueness partly as a result of exposure to conflicting theories and value systems involving appeal to individual loyalty and commitment. Having to decide between conflicting value systems in some hands-on context such as a civil war requires the individual to give at least some thought to what they believe in or 'stand for', even if such reflection is not always very profound. However, having to decide between, say, loyalty to the king or to the republic, where which decision one makes is literally a life-and-death matter, may (and should) bring about more searching self-analysis than the most rigorous seminar or senior common-room discussion.

While this says something about the intensity of self-analysis, it does not consider its range. In a critical state of affairs like that mentioned above, the range of choices narrows to a very small number; there is no place for considering options which are not relevant to the immediate situation. Entertaining a wider range of options is more likely to occur when there is declining social cohesion but reasonable stability which provide individuals with the space to consider the attractions or otherwise of alternative ways of being, and to actualise some of them. Thus the ability to strive for and assert autonomy is dependent both on the context in which individuals find themselves, and on their ability to posit, explore and actualise possible non-actual options.

This is to say something about the *social* context in which autonomy may manifest itself, but what of the interpersonal one? We have said that individuals may or may not regard other human individuals as being 'equally unique selves', and whether or not they do makes a crucial difference to how their autonomy 'cashes out'. It may be possible for strong individuals to act autonomously because they are able to bend others to their will – obstructions are ruthlessly removed, or ignored. In this case we have a very small number of autonomous individuals and a very large number of heteronomous ones, and this has perhaps been the situation throughout much of human history, supported by all manner of theoretical 'justifications' to the effect that this is 'the way things must be', it is 'the natural order of things', that some are 'born to rule' and others to 'be ruled' etc. It is argued that hierarchies are 'necessary', otherwise nothing would be done and chaos would ensue, and this line of argument has been largely accepted by the heteronomous multitude, or they have at least acquiesced to it, having no option but to do so.

Agents and Patients

Another way of talking about this is in terms of the agent/patient distinction. Let us return for a moment to some of the issues discussed in Chapter One, where human consciousness was characterised as a dynamic, changing, creative, purposive system, such that the individual's experience is of incessant desiring which is articulated as purposes – future states of affairs – which can be achieved only by an intricate interweaving of the purposive pathways with the causal networks of the physical dimension of human existence. And we *feel* our way along these pathways in the sense that we are pleased when we succeed in achieving our purposes, and are sad and disappointed when we fail, or when the goal we have striven for turns out not to be what we anticipated. Why we fail or have an unexpected outcome may be because of our own deficiencies, or because of obstruction by the natural course of events, or by other human beings. Our elation at success is the greater if we feel that it is the outcome of our *own* efforts, but so is disappointment at failure; and disappointment is compounded by anger if we consider the failure to have been brought about by another human being either through their carelessness or malevolent intent.

The point is that our *investment* in our own aims is usually greater than in those of others, so that while we are proportionately more pleased when we succeed we are also that much more disappointed when we fail, so that it is tempting and convenient to pre-empt the possibility of such disappointment either or both by not having any aims of our own, or by attributing blame for failure to others. Both of these surely occur with the utmost frequency, and it is the dynamic underlying both the autonomy/heteronomy relation and the agent/patient one. It is risky and dangerous to be autonomous, because one is responsible for generating one's own aims and for their outcome; it is risky and dangerous to be an agent for the same reasons. It is so much easier to allow others to formulate one's aims for one, because then *they* are responsible for unwelcome outcomes, and one may be willing to sacrifice the joys of one's own possible success to achieve this comfort.

However, there is more involved than this because although one may wish to relinquish self-determination in order to avoid its possible unpleasant outcomes, there are occasions on which one *does* wish to act autonomously, to be an agent rather than a patient, and also occasions on which one has no choice but to do so because others thrust autonomy and agency upon one. Thus human consciousness exhibits yet another tension, or perhaps another version of the same tension – that between autonomy and heteronomy or agency and patiency. We like to evade responsibility for difficult situations but *at the same time* we do not wish to be committed to having all our actions dictated to or imposed on us by others.

The next question to ask is how much *choice* we have in the matter – can we genuinely opt for autonomy and agency rather than their opposites if we so decide or is it less clear-cut than this? We have already discussed the distinctions between reasons and causes and actions and behaviour, and seen that in the case of human beings we account for what they do in terms of purposiveness – they have reasons for what they do rather than *being* caused to do it (at least some of the time), so that they can be said to *act* rather than *behave*. The important point is that we confine the term 'act' to a state of affairs which has been brought about by the agent's *initiating* it as a result of deliberation, intention, goal formulation and so on. If the event has been brought about by some antecedent cause or determinant over which the individual has no control, or is ignorant of, we talk of 'behaviour'. The difference between the two is experienced by the individual as 'being in charge', as opposed to 'not being in charge', and on some occasions this is pleasant and on others unpleasant according to whether or not the individual *wishes* to be in charge or not. We wish to be in charge of purposive pathways which are important to us but are happy to abdicate responsibility for difficult or unpleasant tasks, allowing others to 'take control' – sometimes! And this is the problem: we vacillate between wanting to be in charge and wanting to evade so being, but unfortunately it is extraordinarily difficult to pick and choose in the matter; having abdicated responsibility for some of our actions we may well find that we cannot reassume it when we choose.

Daily experience (and vocabulary) is full of examples of this problem: we speak of being 'helpless pawns', or 'ciphers' or 'victims of circumstances', or 'at the will of others', the implication being that we are caught up in some scheme of things which we cannot understand or control. Now, there is something in this, because a good deal of human existence is such that we 'cannot do much about it'. We have no say in our birth and upbringing, very little in our physical/biological make-up: so that any opportunity we have to create ourselves must be in the context of these 'givens'. There would be no point in Woody Allen's ambition to 'be someone else', or at least not in the radical sense of changing these givens, although we *can* do a good deal about what sort of 'someone' we are in the sense of pursuing the sort of life we regard as worthwhile. (This matter of 'givens' may however be changing in for example the case of transsexuals.)

It is in this sense that the agent/patient distinction begins to bite, because our most poignant experience of it is *vis-à-vis others*: it is to other conscious beings that we attribute *deliberate* help or hindrance with our projects. While we may resent being only four feet tall, or that a storm has ruined our prize chrysanthemums, we know that it is pointless to do so, but if we are crippled or disfigured by some hereditary disease we might feel justified in resenting our parents' irresponsibility in reproducing because we consider that they could have chosen to do otherwise. We shall discuss interpersonal relations more fully in the next chapter, but in the present context of the Self we can see that individuals apprehend themselves as either autonomous or heteronomous, or as agents or patients, in terms of whether or not they consider that they *initiate* what they do, and whether or not they are '*in charge*' of it, and while only some of what one does can be under one's control, it is important to us that this part shall be if not under our control, at least controllable by us if we so choose, that is, that we could seize control if it were deemed desirable.

Thus it would seem that we would like to feel that if we choose to be a patient it is because we *have chosen* to be one, not because we had no alternative. Undoubtedly we alternate between the two conditions the whole time, and this is largely in terms of our capacities and vulnerabilities, ie things we are able to do, and things we cannot do, or do not wish to do. Part of the lifelong exercise of achieving self-understanding is establishing for oneself what one can and cannot do, and what one chooses not to do because one prefers to do something else, so that identifying *which* things one wishes to retain under one's control, and which one will leave to others, is part of the juggling act of everyday life. These then are the parameters in terms of which we organise ourselves.

Autonomy/heteronomy and agency/patiency, then, are largely synonymous where one needs to be autonomous to be an agent *and* to decide to be a patient. The intriguing question is whether one can move from heteronomy/patiency by *assuming* autonomy/agency, because if one claims that one can, then surely that means that one *is* already an autonomous agent – otherwise it would not be possible! Perhaps all one can say is that heteronomy/patiency carry within them the *potential* for autonomy/agency, a potential which can be actualised by a self-conscious decision of the individual based on their assessment of their own unique predicament in terms of which aspects *could* be changed or brought under the individual's control, and of how desirable it is that they should be. There can be no rules which dictate on which occasions such decisions should be made, because it is a matter of individual judgment on the individual situation where the ultimate test is whether or not the individual 'feels right' and, as we have seen, this involves considering alternative future possible states of affairs and judging whether or not they should be pursued. There is always an element of risk – the outcome may not be as one has imagined – but the alternative is to avoid making such decisions and remain a heteronomous patient although this may very well 'feel wrong' for the individual. It may well be that one 'feels wrong' about situations which one is powerless to change and where an attitude of *stoicism* in which one tries to feel as little as possible is a natural response. Unfortunately, judging when stoicism is appropriate and when it is not is another difficult decision. Premature stoicism may be easier than striving to change one's situation, or it may be a way of preserving some aspects of one's life which one values and 'putting up with' the rest, for example, keeping one's hated job in order not to lose the income it generates which at least enables one to do *some* of the things one values.

A topical, much-discussed example of this is domestic violence, usually but not always where women and children are the victims. Much thought has been given to trying to resolve the problem, without conspicuous success: the problem very often being the conflict between *loyalty* (to the abuser) and the urgent need for flight from the situation.

So far I have been discussing autonomy/heteronomy and agency/patiency in relation to our notion of Self and suggested that it is part of our sense of selfhood to apprehend ourselves as standing in one or other of these relations *vis-à-vis* the external world and other people. We are aware that we are either *doing* or *being done to*, but this does not tell us which will 'feel right' in any given instance, so that while current thinking suggests that the active rather than the passive relation is both sought and desired on all occasions, this is an oversimplification of a very complex set of considerations. In the next chapter we shall pursue the issue in the context of interpersonal relations, but before doing so there is one final concept which has a bearing on autonomy and agency, and this is Authority.

Authority

In general, authority is experienced as *pressure* on the individual which 'pushes' them along purposive pathways. Its benign face is *guidance*, of helping individuals to pursue their purposes; its malign face is *obstruction* or *oppression*, preventing individuals from doing things they want to do or making them do things they don't want to do. In both cases the pressure is apprehended as external to or outside the individual: they are not the 'author' of it themselves. The three most usual forms of authority are Religious, Political and Professional, and I shall say a little about each of these in order to show how authority in all its forms may be intimately intertwined with both the individual's sense of self and with the actualisation of their own purposes. Religious authority usually takes the form of a body of doctrine which purports to give an account of the nature of things in which a deity or supernatural being is said to be both the creator and legislator of 'all that is' (although this would need to be qualified in the case of eg Buddhism, especially Theravada). How this is to be understood by people in general is either contained in a sacred text and/or is in the hands of a small group of individuals (priests, mullahs, rabbis etc) who 'interpret' the deity's wishes and intentions because these are not considered to be accessible to the uninitiated. For 'believers' (those who accept the doctrine) such interpretations provide welcome and comforting guidance as to how they should conduct their lives; for unbelievers they may be regarded as intrusive, oppressive interference, especially as they are often presented as self-justifying so that objections and criticisms by mere humans are dismissed because God (or whoever) 'moves in mysterious ways', so that one cannot expect to understand 'his purposes'. Certainly within some religions there is considerable latitude for discussion, but the fact remains that religious authority can be very powerful, especially when it is allied with political authority as it has widely been in the past and still is in some parts of the world.

Political authority, likewise, can be seen as offering guidance and protection, or as imposing restrictions. In this case the pressure is reinforced by codified laws and punishment for those who break or disobey them. It is sometimes argued that political authority has been formulated by and hence has the agreement of those on whom it is imposed, but the notion of a 'social contract' (famously formulated by Jean-Jacques Rousseau) is a very muddy one and few would agree either that they have any say in its formulation, or that they are in agreement with its tenets. Most people would consider that political authority is imposed-by-others rather than self-imposed, although they would agree that *some* form of political authority is necessary for the organisation of society. In the present context we can say that individuals experience these two types of authority as pressures on them to think and act in various ways with which they may or may not be in agreement, and we can see that they contribute to moulding the notions which individuals have of themselves because they define themselves, at least in part, in terms of the social setting in which they find themselves. This is not to say that they will necessarily agree with these social forces, but the form their disagreement takes will be influenced by what they are opposing.

Professional authority is a rather different case because it can and should be based on the 'expertise' of the individual(s) to whom it is attributed. Since no human being is omniscient and there is an increasingly enormous amount of information available to us, we have little hope of mastering any of it unless we have access to those who have detailed acquaintance with some particular field. Distinguishing the genuine expert from the charlatan is a difficult matter and we shall make mistakes in this, but since we can only make informed decisions on the basis of information available to us and much of this will come from other people, we have to try. It is tempting to regard *all* authority as essentially antagonistic to the achievement of autonomy and agency, but this is a mistaken understanding of what these involve. What is essential to autonomy and agency is taking a critically analytic attitude to the claims of 'experts', and this involves an incessant effort to listen and reflect which is far more difficult than either rejecting all authoritative pronouncements out of hand, or accepting all of them and letting others do one's thinking for one. Both these reactions are prevalent in present day society and reflect our exasperation with the incomprehensibility and complexity of modern life.

These matters will be explored further in our discussion of Interpersonal Relations in Part Two.

The matters discussed in relation to the Self, especially in relation to society, have also been explored within a sociological perspective by such thinkers and researchers as George Herbert Mead, William Isaac Thomas, Edwin Lemert and Erving Goffman.

Enlightenment is man's emergence from his self-incurred immaturity. Immaturity is the inability to use one's own understanding without the guidance of another. This immaturity is *self-incurred* if its cause is not lack of understanding, but lack of resolution and courage to use it without the guidance of another. The motto of enlightenment is therefore: *Sapere aude!* Have courage to use your *own* understanding!

– Immanuel Kant, 'An Answer to the Question:
"What is Enlightenment?"', in: Kant's Political Writings, ed Hans Reiss, tr
H.B. Nisbet, CUP, 1970, p54

How is it possible to keep one's own way? Constantly some clamour or other calls us aside; rarely does our eye behold anything that does not require us to drop our own preoccupations instantly to help. I know there are a hundred decent and praiseworthy ways of losing *my own way,* and they are truly highly 'moral'! Indeed those who now preach the morality of pity even take the view that precisely this and only this is moral – to lose one's *own* way in order to come to the assistance of one's neighbour. I know just as certainly that I only need to expose myself to the sight of some genuine distress and I am lost. And if a suffering friend said to me, 'Look, I am about to die, please promise to die with me', I should promise it; and the sight of a small mountain tribe fighting for its liberty would persuade me to offer it my hand and my life ... All such arousing of pity and calling for help is secretly seductive, for 'our own way' is too hard and demanding and too remote from love and gratitude of others, and we do not really mind escaping from it – and from our very own conscience – to flee into the conscience of others and into the lovely temple of 'the religion of pity'.

...You will also wish to help – but only those whose distress you *understand* entirely because they share with you one suffering and one hope – your friends – and only in the manner in which you help yourself.

– Friedrich Nietzsche, The Gay Science,
tr Walter Kaufmann, Vintage Books, 1974, pp270, 271

You can recognise those who live for others by the strained look on the faces of the others.

– Iris Murdoch, on a BBC Radio Three programme,
paraphrasing C.S. Lewis' The Screwtape Letters

PART TWO
INTERPERSONAL RELATIONS

3

AUTONOMY AND ALTRUISM

F ROM THE PREVIOUS DISCUSSIONS OF THE activities of consciousness and of the self, we are beginning to see the emergence of a fundamental tension in human consciousness between the desire to act autonomously and the desire to be 'together' with other human beings, the latter involving some abdication of autonomy.

In this chapter, we shall explore these further by saying something about the 'binding' phenomenon of *sympathy* where we are *affected by* the feelings and desires of others, though not in any straightforward way because, while we are *affected* by the feeling-states of others, we are unsure how to *respond* to them.

The varieties of sympathy have been very thoroughly discussed by Max Scheler in *The Nature of Sympathy* (1923), and it is worth noting that today 'sympathy' is often taken to be roughly synonymous with 'empathy' which in turn is taken to mean 'trying to imagine how the other feels', and hence respond accordingly.

Our discussion in Part One has identified *imagining* as the means by which we can re-visit the past and anticipate the future, as well as experience the actual world in a way which enables us to attend to particular details *of* actual experience, 'lifted', as it were, from relentless temporality. We have also seen that *desiring* (some future state-of-affairs) 'keeps us going' through the formulation of *purposes* which we strive to achieve by *willing*.

In our interpersonal relations, we endeavour to 'relate' to one another by 'imagining' how others might 'feel' to be another, different person, as a preliminary to – or as part of – deciding to interact with them. This effort is fraught with difficulties because others are inalienably *other* and inaccessible to us, at least partially. But we *do* consider that some access is possible because we feel interested in them and realize that they *affect* us. Unless one is a hermit, we unavoidably encounter them and need to devise strategies for dealing with such encounters. Such 'interest' in others is sometimes hostile, sometimes affectionate – we *want* to avoid them, or to spend more time with them.

And we are aware of the *suffering* of others which we take to be analogous to our own suffering, inevitable, at least some of the time, because of our embodied sensate natures, and we want to alleviate it: sometimes.

But, because we are all different individuals, we cannot be sure that we have correctly identified either the nature of the suffering or the suitable alleviation. We constantly vacillate between attraction towards others and wariness of them (they could harm us). This is the constantly reiterated *tension*.

How do we deal with it? I suggest that it would be better to avoid a hasty 'knee-jerk' response in which we assume, probably incorrectly, that the other is experiencing what *we* would feel, and also avoid attempting to bring about the alleviation *we* would like if we were them; which we are not.

What is the alternative? Perhaps by a stance of *imaginative* sympathy which involves a serious attempt to try, as far as possible, to put ourselves in the place of the other – always incomplete – and respond with caution. It is very easy to get it wrong, and misguided sympathy and 'help' may well be regarded as *interference*.

Realising this attempt is not in fact entirely possible leads one to appreciate the *alterity* or radical heterogeneity or unique individuality of the other, and hence makes one even more cautious about 'helping', especially given the prevalence of *grumbling* – where grumblers wish only to grumble rather than do anything about their situation, or be 'helped' to alleviate it. As King Gama says in the Gilbert and Sullivan opera *Princess Ida*:

O don't the days seem lank and long

When all goes right and nothing goes wrong,
And isn't your life extremely flat
With nothing whatever to grumble at.

We can learn to ignore the jeremiads of the professional grumbler – eventually!

These observations suggest that 'blanket' solutions to suffering should be avoided, except in the case of obvious physical suffering where a piece of sticking plaster, an aspirin and a cup of tea or a pat on the hand may be enough; although in the case of more serious suffering from injury or disease, more radical medical alleviation is necessary.

As Nietzsche observed in the passage quoted at the beginning of this chapter, we only stand any chance of 'getting it right' with those we know well; furthermore, excessive concern with others diverts us from the pursuit of autonomy, the other aspect of our tension.

Thus, the problems with sympathy are a) identification of the feeling-states of others and b) the problem of how to *respond*, even if the identification has been correct. What of *psychological* suffering? We shall say more about this later in the chapter.

Sympathy: Emotional Infection and Imaginative Sympathy

In general, because of this tension between the *belonging* appeal and the *individuating or differentiating* appeal, our stances towards *others* vacillate between treating-as-the-same and treating-as-different, and because it can be very difficult to ascertain in what respects others are different, we may tend to assume that they are 'like oneself' and project inappropriate feelings and desires onto them. Only very close acquaintance gives one any chance of 'getting it right' and even then one can still make mistakes. Thus, what is regarded as a centrally 'natural' human action of 'helping others' is fraught with many problems.

The issues are again nicely summarised by Nietzsche in one of his most trenchant passages, quoted at the beginning of this chapter. In spite of the usual Nietzschean hyperbole, there are some very serious points in this passage: a) the temptation to lose oneself in others' problems because it is easier and has the added bonus of earning one the praise and gratitude of others, b) the importance of helping only those one *understands* (or are closer to understanding), c) the difficulty of following one's own way, partly because it is difficult to ignore the appeals of others, partly because one is often very unclear as to what one's own way *is*.

Before leaving the topic of sympathy we need to say something about 1) responses which are not the 'natural' ones to the feeling-states of others and 2) responses to feeling-states other than suffering.

In the first consideration, we can say that our discussion so far has concentrated on the suffering/help nexus because this is the everyday understanding of the term 'sympathy', but it is important to note that while most people may consider it 'natural' to respond to apprehended suffering with attempts to alleviate that suffering – and we have seen that this can be a perilous business – some individuals may be quite indifferent to such suffering, and yet others may *enjoy* it and seek to extend and intensify it. While our reaction to these two types of effects may be that they are those only of 'sick' individuals, they are, nonetheless, quite common. We have already seen that indifference to the suffering of those with whom we are not acquainted is fairly usual; while we may act to help a stranger who crosses our path, we do not seek out those who do not, nor do we spend very much time feeling concerned about them – a special effort has to be made. In modern society we are urged to be concerned about those in other parts of the world and we do make some effort to do this, if only by giving some money to an earthquake appeal, for example, but most people, understandably, feel that they do not have the time and energy to do much more than this: it is fully taken up by the people they do know, and for whom they feel some affection and responsibility.

Indifference to the suffering of those whom we *do* know is regarded as 'unnatural' but may be the result of self-absorption or of the view that one should not 'interfere'. As we have seen, such a view may or may not be justified; if it is the outcome of reflection on the matter then it may well be justified, but one can decide only as a result of considering the specific situation. Such decisions are likely to be condemned as callous or 'unfeeling', and individuals taking them need to be confident that they are the right ones. Often we have no such confidence!

Indifference to suffering shades over an uneasy borderline into *enjoyment* of suffering. Certainly we may feel justified in taking pleasure in the suffering of others when it is regarded as a case of the other 'getting their comeuppance' or their 'just deserts', when the other has behaved in a way we disapprove of which causes pain to others, or is regarded as exhibiting excessive pride or self-importance. *Schadenfreude* is a very common response surely experienced by everyone at some time, but more difficult to account for is deliberate cruelty of which torture is the most extreme form. A great deal of attention has been given to 'man's inhumanity to man' at the end of the twentieth century and also now in the twenty-first, but no satisfactory explanation of it appears to be forthcoming. We deplore it but recognise it as a very deep-seated feature of human beings which continues to manifest itself however 'civilised' we consider ourselves to be. This is the unacceptable face of sympathy – if we were not aware that others suffer there would be no point in treating them cruelly. There is little satisfaction from 'mistreating' a stone or a block of wood because they cannot 'feel', although there is some short-lived satisfaction of the letting-off-steam variety to be gained from, for example, kicking one's car when it will not start on a snowy morning or stops at a crucial moment (as, memorably, in an episode of the TV series *Fawlty Towers*).

But how do we account for more 'full blooded' enjoyment of inflicting suffering on others? It is not only the professional torturer who does this; it occurs in many interpersonal situations, particularly domestic ones, as the novels of Ivy Compton-Burnett compellingly chronicle. Husbands and wives, parents and children, masters and servants can all inflict horrible damage on one another in the full knowledge that they are doing so, and the more close the ties between the individuals concerned, the more intense the suffering can be. What can one say about this? There are two possible lines of explanation: a) that individuals enjoy the exercise of *power* over one another because it reinforces and strengthens their sense of self-esteem – in the conflict of individual wills they consider that they have 'won' if they make another suffer as it is a way of diminishing the other's power; and b) individuals damage one another because they are not *chez soi*: they are filled with *resentment*, that is, they consider that others have deprived them of the satisfaction of their desires and obstructed them in the fulfilment of their purposes, and consequently they wish to *punish* them.

We can see that a) and b) go some way to offering explanations of interpersonal conflict but do not account for inflicting suffering on those not known to one, or those whom one has no possible reason to resent. Perhaps all one can say is that *cruelty* or *sadism* is a feature of human beings which can be expressed irrespective of the justification for it, or of the deserts of the victim. The impersonal exercise of power can be a source of satisfaction because of the fragility of individuals' sense of selfhood, and when this is combined with our awareness that others have the power to hurt *us*, a 'pre-emptive strike' makes some sort of sense. On the political level the inanities and insanities of the Cold War provide ample evidence of how easy it is to turn defensive acts into offensive ones once paranoia has gained a hold, and this is mirrored in interpersonal relations. The absence of *trust* between individuals is responsible for all manner of barbarous and indefensible actions which the individuals concerned would no doubt themselves condemn if they reflected on the matter. The problem is that human beings are subject to so many demands and desires that they can rarely act in the way they would like to, instead allowing themselves to be caught up in responses they do not like because they lack confidence in themselves and are wary and fearful of others.

Thus, it seems, indifference to and enjoyment of the suffering of others may have all manner of 'justifications', many of them understandable if not *genuinely* justifiable. Given the fragility of both individuals' sense of themselves and of their understanding of the world and other people, it is scarcely surprising that although they have the capacity to alleviate one another's suffering, and even *want* to do so on many occasions, they ignore or compound it as often or not, justifying doing so in terms of threats to themselves which must be countered by threats to others. And the dynamic of these types of responses is predicated on our apprehension of human *vulnerability*. When we are fearful we are likely to act viciously lest we be overwhelmed by the other(s), and these responses have disconcerting parallels in the world of non-human animals where a threatened creature will respond with tooth and claw. Humans, too, respond with tooth and claw although not always physically, because our higher levels of consciousness have armed us with an arsenal of verbal and psychological weapons which can be every bit as effective.

As we shall see in later discussions in this chapter, it is interesting to note the prevalence of military metaphors in talking about interpersonal relations (and in fact human relations at all levels), which suggests that much human experience is apprehended as beleaguered; that our 'feeling vulnerable' nature is such that we regard ourselves as under constant threat of 'invasion' from other humans, and from the world in which we find ourselves. To think of human nature in this way, with the emphasis on feeling and desiring rather than on reasoning, makes a good deal of difference both to how we try to explain ourselves to ourselves, and to how we respond to other human beings and to the non-human world. However high an opinion we may have of ourselves, this vulnerability cannot be overlooked; or if it is, as it has been by some thinkers, such as Kant, we arrive only at a distorted and misleading picture of human nature.

Even a quick survey of the amount and varieties of suffering in the world (through war, famine, disease, natural disasters such as earthquakes or tsunamis) can fill us with sadness, desperation, despair... such that more positive experience is overshadowed and receives far less attention.

Sympathy and Feeling-states Other than Sympathy

By this stage the reader may feel that the picture of the early 21st century *individual* emerging in this account is a rather gloomy one – the individual is isolated, lonely, misunderstood, un-understandable, capable of inflicting or receiving underserved suffering, wrestling with impossible struggles for self-understanding and for the attainment of difficult-to-formulate and even-more-difficult-to-obtain goals which, even if achieved, may well not turn out to be as anticipated! However, this is only one side of the picture. So far there has been perhaps undue emphasis on *negative* feeling and on suffering, partly because a good deal of human experience can contain these, and partly because the theories of self-congratulatory pessimists, such as Schopenhauer, the arch-pessimist, have been very influential in encouraging us to think this way. To do so is apparently to be tough-minded and realistic, and not to do so is to be naïve and even simple-minded. But there *is* positive and life-enhancing experience, although this has received very little philosophical attention, Nietzsche, perhaps the arch-optimist, being a notable exception, and we need to say something about it in the context of 'sympathy' because just as unpleasant feeling-states can be communicated, so can pleasant ones; and not only are they communicated but they can 'move' others. So is their neglect something to do with there being an asymmetry between them and painful ones, which make it unnecessary to discuss them?

At the end of the passage quoted earlier Nietzsche says: 'I want to make them bolder, more persevering, simpler, gayer. I want to teach them what is understood by so few today, least of all by these preachers of pity: *to share not suffering but joy*' (*The Gay Science*, p271).

At first sight there would appear to be plenty of positive feeling-states ie ones which we enjoy and wish to pursue, although, as we shall see, making a distinction between 'positive' and 'negative' is problematic if one tries to establish a one-one correspondence between them and specific feeling-states. However, let us make a start by saying that states which we pursue and enjoy are laughter, delight, felicity, interest, happiness, enthusiasm, excitement, curiosity, ie those states which make us 'feel alive', *wanting to continue with* whatever situation or activity it is which seems to generate them. The 'desire to continue with' is important because it points up the contrast between life-*enhancing* and life-*denying* (Nietzsche's *ja-sagender* and *nein-sagender*) states, and it is surely the former which 'keep us going' while the latter make us 'grind to a halt'. If we are interested in, enthusiastic about, enjoying an activity, this provides us with the energy to continue, whereas if we are fearful or angry or bored we do not wish to continue, we wish to 'go away from' whatever it is, or wish it to go away from us.

Now, what has this to do with 'sympathy' and other-regardingness? We do not seem to need others in these cases in the same way as we do with suffering. There is no 'natural' way to respond to the joy or enthusiasm of others except to wish them well or perhaps join them in their enthusiasm. The answer is that it depends on the specific situation or activity. What is certain is that individuals can block or obstruct activities which others are enjoying, either because they obstruct their own purposes or from sheer vindictiveness, but is there any 'positive' response that seems to accompany recognition of a life-enhancing feeling-state in another? Just as misery can 'infect' others, so can joy, but what then? One may join in the dance, but reflecting on the joy of others may require nothing more in the way of response than helping to ensure that it continues without impediment. Certainly reflection may show one either that there are ways of involving oneself to enhance the joy, or that the joy of the other is not justified – eg the delight of the criminal in successfully 'pulling off a job' – in which case one may be moved to act in order to make sure that the joy is short-lived.

Thus, we can say that life-enhancing feeling-states are communicated, and that, as with suffering, we may not *share* them – although there are situations where enjoyment *is* surely shared, eg having a few drinks with friends – but we do *recognise* them, and some type of response may be appropriate and, although such responses receive far less attention than 'doing good' in the case of suffering, they may well require careful reflection and thoughtfully judged action. Promoting joyful situations by preventing them from being spoiled or terminated is *as* important as alleviating suffering. This is a supremely important observation because so much attention has been given to responses to suffering that we tend to forget that it would be far preferable to *prevent* suffering in the first place wherever it is possible.

Part of the reason why less attention has been given to enhancing what we might call felicity-states than to alleviating suffering is that they have always had a dubious moral status, being regarded as 'less serious', 'frivolous', 'shallow', 'empty-headed' and so on, and this view has been encouraged by much religious thinking, and by philosophers influenced by them (eg Kant's reference to 'something altogether more high-minded than happiness', ie *duty*). It is not difficult to appreciate why this has been so in the past when human existence was frequently perilous in the extreme, because human beings had little control over any of the dangers and threats from the physical world, their own fragility, and the depredations of others. Consequently, those who tried to understand the human condition took it as given that human life would always be a vale of tears, and offered what comfort they could by postulating a deity who understood things better than they did, and a 'life after death' which offered the proper and only prospect of felicity. To expect to enjoy very much of earthly existence was regarded as unrealistic and dangerous – unrealistic because such joys as there might be were doomed to be short-lived, and dangerous because it distracted attention from propitiating

the deity in order to ensure a 'place in heaven'. In addition, human effort
was required to survive at all in a hostile physical world containing equally
hostile other humans.

Although human beings now have more control over the physical world,
and, to a lesser extent, over themselves and others, this type of thinking
continues to have a very strong hold on the picture they have of the nature
of things. We have seen that human beings continue to be physically
vulnerable because of their sentient embodied nature, and the increasing
sophistication of human consciousness means that they are more rather
than less psychologically vulnerable than they were in the past because
they have higher expectations and more complex purposes. Given this, it is
scarcely surprising that the human psyche appears to be programmed to
expect the worst, and that switching to another mode, even as modest a
one as hoping for the best, much less one of expecting and promoting the
best, is likely to to be very difficult! This is not just because of human
intransigence but because working out a mode of being which actively
pursues the promotion of felicity-states and human *flourishing*, rather than
repairing damage already done, needs a great deal of adjustment and
reflection – in fact, possibly a complete overhaul of our views of the human
condition which questions what we have taken as 'givens', proposes
alternative presuppositions, and thinks through their implications. This is
a tall order, especially as we may be only at the very beginning of such a
task (as Thomas Nagel puts it, 'Even the most civilized human beings have
only a haphazed understanding of how to live'), and will be discouraged
from its pursuit by the self-congratulatory pessimists already mentioned,
who will be quick to pour cold water on any such pursuit. (Thomas Nagel,
The View from Nowhere, OUP, 1986, p186.)

More will be said about this in Chapter Four, under the heading 'The
Recalibrated Individual'; for the present we need to be clear only about the
connection between the communication of feeling-states between human
individuals and suffering and felicity. It has been pointed out that while we
may be moved to alleviate apprehended suffering in others, we may equally
be moved to promote or at least prevent obstruction to felicity, but that
this latter receives far less attention than the former. The important point
at issue is that promotion of felicity may well *prevent* suffering, so that

there would be far less need to address ourselves to its alleviation. In addition, we need to think again about what we mean by felicity, a useful word, and see that it is *not* synonymous with 'pleasure', which is often considered to mean 'mere pleasure' ie a shallow, worthless, frivolous condition. If we regard felicity as synonymous with the life-enhancing or with human flourishing, we are nearer to giving the type of seriousness it surely deserves, and then we can include 'the worthwhile', which brings out its connection with the central issues of this book, that is, the encouragement and development of individual creative potential.

It is surely the case that if individuals have the opportunity to express their individual potential by formulating and pursuing their *own* purposes and fulfilling their own desires rather than those of others imposed on them against their will, then they will regard these activities as worthwhile. If they regard them as worthwhile, then they are life-enhancing (one justifiably wishes to *continue* with them), and that in turn gives rise to felicity-states which are experienced as thoroughly serious and meaningful rather than frivolous and insignificant. If this is the dynamic of felicity-states then they cannot be dismissed as less important than suffering and its alleviation. And, as far as other-regardingness is concerned, the promotion of such states in others (as well as in oneself) is as important as the alleviation of already-experienced suffering: although it is still necessary to expose and eliminate *hitherto unrecognised* sources or cases of suffering, indeed an ongoing and unending task.

Thus sympathy can involve a good deal more than its usual understanding suggests. We have said that one cannot find a one-one correspondence between specific feeling-states and points on a positive/negative spectrum, and we now need to say more about this claim. It is sometimes assumed that certain feeling-states are negative and others positive – that eg anger and fear are negative and happiness and freedom from suffering are positive, but this is not correct, because whether or not one regards the feeling-state as the one or the other can be determined only relative to *the context* in which it occurs.

If, instead of thinking of specific emotions as positive or negative in terms of whether or not they are enjoyable or painful, we think instead of whether or not what we are doing is life-enhancing or life-denying, then specific emotions which accompany the activity can be regarded as either positive or negative in *this* sense. Thus fear or anger may be positive in that they promote our activity; joy or enthusiasm may interfere with it, especially if they are intensely experienced. Do we not find a state of euphoria often makes it difficult to concentrate although it may function as a spur to the activity, whereas being in a temper may galvanise us to extra effort to achieve some purpose although it could also distract us from it. We can say then that it is only by being acquainted with the *context* in question, including the purposes aimed at, that we can decide the status of our feeling-states, and that in general they are neutral until assessed in context.

The relevance of these observations to our discussion of sympathy is that they reinforce the importance of being very clear about not only the feeling-states of others but also about their individual characteristics, and the contexts in question. It is frequently observed that some individuals 'thrive on stress' while others disintegrate under it, and this is correct as far as it goes – which is not very far, because what sort of stress in what situation makes a difference. The ruthless business man who operates effortlessly professionally may fall apart under problems in his private life; the reclusive intellectual may amaze everyone by rising to the occasion in an emergency, or by acting very decisively when their vital interests are affected. Thus we would be mistaken to either categorise other individuals as being of a particular 'type' with such and such characteristics – individuals may constantly (re)create themselves either *intentionally* or *un*intentionally – or to assume that we will know how they will respond in specific situations, and consequently that we will 'know how they feel'. Nine times out of ten, we do not, and we should avoid the temptation to invest them with responses *we* would most likely have in their situation. Not only do we not know how they feel, we also do not know what status to attribute to the feeling-states we assume them to be experiencing without very careful consideration of the situation and also discussion with *them* as to how they regard what is happening to them, if this is available. This last issue will be pursued later in the next chapter when we come to 'conversation'.

Finally, before leaving this topic, it is worth noting that programmes for human improvement often work with very simple-minded assumptions about what people want/need based on all manner of confused and mistaken views about human nature. Even apparently self-evident improvements such as reducing starvation and illness are not without their problems, though an emergency status may well be assigned to a specific situation as the only appropriately humane response. During the course of this book it will hopefully emerge that social and political decisions can be generated *only* by the contributions of the individuals concerned, and that such individuals can only make informed contributions if they have clarified for *themselves* what it is that they desire and what they consider a worthwhile life to be. If this is so, then the contribution each of us makes to *others* may well be to create a climate in which such individual flourishing is possible, and *not* to interfere by assuming that 'we know best'. With this in mind let us now turn to consideration of a notion frequently linked with sympathy, that is, *altruism.*

Altruism, Benevolence, Respect

It is commonly assumed that we should be sensitive to the experience and feeling-states of others and that, at least on some occasions, we should put our own desires and purposes aside in favour of others. Not to do so is regarded as 'unfeeling', 'callous', 'selfish', and to be 'self*less*' in the sense of 'always thinking of others' is highly regarded in our folk wisdom. (An extreme example of this can be found in May Sinclair's novel *Harriett Frean*, discussed in Part Three.) The discussion in the previous section has shown some of the difficulties of these assumptions, and we shall now cover some of the same ground though from a slightly different perspective by looking at 'altruism'. This is usually contrasted with 'egoism' in philosophical discussion, where one considers whether, for example, all actions, however much they may appear to be other-regarding, in fact are fundamentally 'selfish', in that the individual engages in them 'for their own benefit' (enlightened self-interest) – the person who plunges into the torrent to rescue a drowning child is actually doing so for their own greater glory, is a usual example.

To again refer to the Nietzsche quotation at the beginning of this Part of the book, individuals who respond to the appeals of others may *lose their own way.* We may add to this the effect on 'the helped' which, as we have seen, may turn out to be 'more of a hindrance than a help' on some or even many occasions. As the character Screwtape writes in C.S. Lewis' *The Screwtape Letters*, 'A sensible human once said, ... "She's the sort of woman who lives for others – you can always tell the others by their hunted expression."' (*The Screwtape Letters*, Collins, 2012, p145.) Thus an over-preoccupation with the welfare of others distracts us from our own pathways, but it may also be a waste of the individual's time, and a source of irritation and obstruction to the 'helped'. If this is so, what is one to say about the widely held view that other-regardingness and altruism are 'a good thing'? Is one to conclude that one should take *no* account of the experience of others, or is it that we need to revise how we understand these terms? Thus it is not a choice between the Scylla of complete selflessness and the Charybdis of complete self-centredness, but rather a delicately balanced responsiveness to others in which reflection on specific situations is a primary requirement rather than the formulating and following of mechanical 'rules' which claim to hold for all occasions. It is not a case of 'always put others first', or of 'look after number one', although there is a tempting simplicity about such maxims which encourage one to abandon having to think too hard about one's actions.

It has been pointed out that there is an absurdity about the 'always put others first' maxim in that if everyone followed it no-one would think about themselves, and it would be a case of 'taking in one another's washing'. This is surely correct, and given the difficulties outlined, it would be a very unwise maxim to follow, so perhaps it is just as well that it is unlikely that more than a small number of people would ever do so. Nonetheless it has a very widespread appeal such that we are made to feel guilty if we do not subscribe to it, and this is the problem: if it is absurd in its more extreme formulation, how is it to be revised to take better account of the expression of unique individuality? The trouble is that the more extreme formulation is the one which has the strongest hold on individuals, whereas a more moderate one is far more appropriate. It is certainly not the case that we can or should ignore others; we cannot help being affected by them, nor should we wish not to be, because our interaction with others can be a source of much that is worthwhile, quite apart from the fact that even if we try to ignore others this is no guarantee that they will ignore us, as we have seen in our discussion of Agents and Patients and Autonomy.

But can we not take account of others without feeling obliged to make their concerns our own? Of course we can, because we do so much of the time, but the difficulty is that this frequently occurs in a rather unstructured way: we are unclear about which features of others should concern us; when it is appropriate to abandon our own projects in favour of those of others; how to choose between 'deserving cases'; how to keep to one's own way in the face of so much suffering and disaster which calls on us to 'do something to help'. The media constantly bombard us with 'worst scenario' situations which have the effect of devastating the kind-hearted and boring the insensitive, so that one wonders what could possibly be an appropriate response to such universal horror. There are no quick and easy answers, but the realisation that *nobody* knows the answers may encourage us to make an attempt to think about whether or not the human condition *must* be so frightful for so many people for so much of the time. The cautiously optimistic line of argument in this book is that it *need not be*, but that making that possible requires a massive re-thinking of our views about ourselves, most particularly by making it as important to promote flourishing as to relieve suffering. In the present context, our understanding of altruism needs to be adjusted to a *tempered altruism*, ie to mean something less demanding than 'always putting others first', and I suggest that the terms *benevolence* and *respect* might be more fitting because they have the connotations of being more general and arms-length than altruism, while retaining the notion that we 'take account of' others, but only to the extent that we recognise their *alterity*, ie that they *differ* from us and do not necessarily share our desires and purposes, although there may be considerable overlap *on some occasions.*

Benevolence, literally 'well-wishing', seems a modest enough stance to take to others, and makes positively obstructing them 'off-limits' except in specific contexts, while not committing one to taking any very great interest in their affairs unless invited to do so. Similarly, 'respect' suggests maintaining some 'distance' between oneself and others, once again, except in specific contexts where one can be reasonably sure that proximity is appropriate and welcome. This proposal may suggest that abdicating or shrugging off responsibility is being recommended, and this is so, but in its defence one can point out that 'taking responsibility for' is very difficult to distinguish from 'interference' and 'patronage' on many occasions – they are very frequently confused! This is not to claim that such a revised stance is easy to achieve – it is exceedingly difficult – and modern society contains multifarious instances of individuals' struggles to disentangle themselves from one another. As we have seen, the tension between the desire to belong and to individuate is ever present in human consciousness, and battles will continue to be waged along these lines for the foreseeable future. What is being suggested here is that the repressive bonds of the altruism demand – experienced by giver and recipient alike – might be loosened by replacing it with the benevolence/respect stance, because to do so increases the 'space' between individuals without inviting them to take no account of one another, even if that were possible, which it is not. Some form of interdependence is here to stay, so we need to work out what form it takes, however daunting the task may be.

We shall say more about this in the next section when we consider Civility, Acquaintance, Friendship and Love. The point is that human individuals cannot possibly respond to all the demands made on them (see for example endless professional charity appeals), so that if they do not organise their responses they will be torn apart by impossible appeals to their feelings; thus it is understandable that a response to this is to cauterise themselves so that they feel as little as possible, and the stiff upper lip is the most common example of this.

To continue our discussion of the tension, let us look at:

Civility, Acquaintance, Friendship, Love

The picture of human consciousness which is beginning to emerge by this time is one of individuated, sentient, self-conscious entities which have a number of capacities or activities which interact constantly with one another to provide us with what we take human experience to be. We are aware of ourselves as loci of incessant desires which articulate themselves as purposes to be satisfied in some future state of affairs over which we consider we have at least partial control. Consequently we apprehend ourselves as constructing or *creating* ourselves from the raw materials of our desires and our interaction with the world of physical objects, and of other living individuals, some of them human like ourselves. Seeing ourselves *as* individuals means that we regard ourselves as discrete entities *separated* from the other furniture of the world, that is, we consider that our individuated state means that there are *boundaries* between ourselves and our surroundings, but while these boundaries separate us from them, they also enable us to *make contact* with them. While these boundaries have a physical aspect – we can literally touch other physical entities, and make other physical contact with them – they also have a non-physical aspect which is difficult to define but is a very important feature of our sense of ourselves. It is as though we have a non-physical penumbra surrounding us which we are aware of as 'ours' or 'part of us', and which on occasion we allow to be breached, and on other occasions vigorously defend against invasion if we feel that our selfhood is being threatened. The contemporary term 'personal space' alludes to this.

We have already noted the fashionable prevalence of military metaphors in talking about the self, and accounted for this in terms of the fragility of our sense of self. We feel that we can easily lose this, and that the experience is unpleasant and thus to be avoided. At the same time, we long to decrease the *loneliness* of the individuated state, and so invite proximity with other individuals, especially other human individuals, because – briefly – this decreases the isolation and vulnerability. Thus we speak of 'invasion', 'siege', 'defences', 'surrender', 'breaching of boundaries' and so on when we try to give an account of human interaction. It is another way of talking about the belonging/individuating tension, and one which highlights the ambivalence and vacillation we experience constantly in our interpersonal relations. The point is that we want *both* to belong (to feel human warmth and closeness) and to be independent of the 'downside' of such belonging ('suffocation', oppression, obstruction of our purposes or trajectories). Is there any way of achieving both or are we condemned to eternal vacillation between the two? The answer is probably that we are so condemned but that the experience of the tension might not be quite so painful if its inevitability is *recognised*, because that will at least relieve us of feeling that there is something wrong with us due to the tension appearing to be irresolvable (as we see in the 'disordered mind/individual' discussion in Chapter Four).

We have already seen that all human beings experience the tension between belonging and individuating; some, perhaps, are scarcely conscious of it, others chronically so, feeling that their lives are blighted by isolation at one end of the scale or by suffocating oppression at the other. And since the way we treat one another contributes crucially to these experiences, it is important to give some thought to the effect we have on others in even the most trivial encounters. A smile and a friendly word may make the day of a lonely person, a brusque dismissal may ruin the day of a sensitive one, but normally we play by ear such encounters because we are preoccupied with our own affairs and with our more absorbing interactions with those we know well. It may be thought that this is the way it has to be – life's too short, etc – and this is probably correct, but at the same time how we treat casually encountered others reflects and is reflected in our stances towards those who are more important to us. Thus, although it is impossible to formulate any rules or even any but the most general maxims, we might say that benevolence and respect as a general stance cashes out as *civility* in our casual interactions with others. By this is meant that we show a basic consideration to others – standing aside for them in the street, picking up a dropped object, exchanging a word – all the activities recommended by the Boy Scout and Girl Guide movements of the past which may now be viewed with derision but which are still regarded as 'automatic' at least by many of the older generation.

Civility

While many Feminists may regard men who hold open car doors, walk on the outside of the pavement, and doff caps as male chauvinists, there are surely modern equivalents of these rituals which are gender-blind or -free and which merely express respect and consideration, rather than patronising 'superiority'. And it is these minimal responses which surely are undemanding and unintrusive but which enable us to operate in a pleasant rather than a surly climate; and this is Civility – evidence of a 'civilised' society, or at least a necessary if not a sufficient condition of it. Certainly a society in which some individuals are treated with less respect than others, of which South African apartheid was a notorious example, as well as the treatment of African-Americans in the Southern States of America, is not one we would want to call civilised, although there are less obvious ways of being disrespectful, so that those who have the most beautiful 'manners' in public may well behave appallingly in private, as we have seen in our discussion of the Hypocrite in Chapter Two.

Acquaintance

This 'involves' us with others a little more than Civility because we may take more interest in and make an effort to help those we come across, sometimes for long periods such as neighbours, sometimes briefly or intermittently such as shop assistants or plumbers or car mechanics. Once again, little is required of us beyond bare courtesy plus a little warmth and friendliness. In some instances, though, this can shade into Friendship or even Love.

Friendship

Let us now turn to Friendship, the interpersonal relation which makes far more demands on us than Civility or Acquaintance, and which is probably regarded, along with Love, as a centrally important feature of human experience. The first thing to say about it is that it should be distinguished from *Acquaintance* although frequently confused with it, very much to its detriment. Some people claim to have 'dozens (or even hundreds) of friends' but it seems likely that most of these should be regarded as 'acquaintances' because it is not within the power of any individual to have the degree of involvement friendship demands with more than a very few individuals. If we return for a moment to the notion of 'boundaries', a Venn-type diagram may help us to think about what is involved in the four notions under discussion.

CIVILITY   ACQUAINTANCE   FRIENDSHIP   LOVE

My suggestion is that in the case of friendship the boundaries between the individuals concerned are partially dissolved or perhaps *perforated* so that we allow our selfhood to be invaded by the individuality of the other to the extent of concerning ourselves with their desires, purposes and well-being in a similar way to which we are concerned with our own. Thus we are prepared, some of the time, to put aside our own purposes in favour of those of the other, or to join them in projects we share with them; we are prepared to trust them with private information about ourselves, and to treat confidentially private information they give us about themselves; we are prepared to defend them against attack, and to help them when they are in trouble. And we do all this because we have affection and liking for them, regarding them as more important than those we do not regard as friends; in fact we regard them as almost as important as ourselves. We need to note the qualifications in this characterisation – 'some of the time', 'almost as important as' – that is, we *partially* identify with them, but not completely. There will be parts of their natures and activities to which we do not have access (though other friends may) and which we do not share, in the sense either of finding such aspects interesting, or of importance to ourselves.

The impartiality of Moral Law, ie treating everyone as *the same*, as Lawrence A. Blum argues in *Friendship, Altruism and Morality*, is at odds with the demands of friendship. Friendship thus characterised is seen as demanding and hazardous. It pulls us towards the belonging end of the spectrum by offering warmth and closeness at the same time as the threat of suffocation and obstruction of our own purposes. It is not surprising therefore that 'keeping one's friends' is a tricky enterprise, unless we have a high degree of indifference to them when it is more appropriate to see them as acquaintances. This passage from E.M. Forster's *Howards End* charts some of the perils of friendship as well as any I know:

> Was Mrs Wilcox one of those unsatisfactory people – there are many of them – who dangle intimacy and then withdraw it? They evoke our interests and affections and keep the life of the spirit dawdling round them. Then they withdraw. When physical passion is involved, there is a definite name for such behaviour – flirting – and if carried far enough it is punishable by law. But no law – not public opinion even – punishes those who coquette

with friendship, though the dull ache they inflict, the sense of misdirected effort and exhaustion, may be as intolerable. Was she one of these?

– *Howards End*, Penguin, 1967, p75

What this passage brings out is the *responsibilities* of friendship, that if one picks people up and puts them down again at whim, one can inflict a great deal of suffering because the other has allowed one to 'cross or breach' the boundaries of their selfhood, so that to withdraw from them is akin to their losing a part of themselves. We speak of a 'rupture' in a friendship and this is a telling term: it can be as violent and as painful. At the same time, too great an invasion of the other can be experienced as equally painful and unacceptable because in this case, rather than a rupture of selfhood, there is an overwhelming and displacement of it, so that the other feels that they have lost such individuality as they had – it has been replaced by the individuality of the 'friend'.

Perhaps this account sounds over-dramatic, and many people would say that they do not experience these problems with their friendships. Undoubtedly it will vary from one individual to another but this is surely evidence for the main point being made in this chapter, which is that precisely where individuals find themselves on the belonging/individuating spectrum or continuum *will* vary from one to another, but that the tension is there. Some individuals may value belonging over individuating and hence experience no difficulty with being 'invaded' by others – they find it a source of comfort; those who value individuating over belonging may claim to prefer to be 'loners' and be prepared to accept the concomitant isolation; but there are many individuals in between who want the advantages of *both* and do not know how to *organise* themselves to achieve them. We have already seen in some detail that it is not possible to achieve only the advantages of both and leave behind the disadvantages, and that the only way of responding to this realization is to *recognise* it.

Certainly it may be possible to adjust one's thinking and actions to take account of the recognition, but this must be a matter of individual reflection; there can be no legislation on the matter because that would presuppose a greater similarity between individuals than exists. We have seen that attempting to treat individuals as 'the same' can lead to disastrous consequences, because to ignore or suppress the incessant creative diversity of human consciousness is a futile exercise. If there can be no legislation on the matter, it is the responsibility of the individual to decide on their own preferences, and the only general claim that is being made is that this is better accomplished in a climate of respect for alterity.

The relevance of these observations to friendship should now be clear. If we find value in closeness to others but wish to retain our selfhood, the realisation that there *is* a tension between the two must structure our reflections. What specific decisions we make will depend on our own self-understanding, and on our understanding of specific others. There are no easy solutions, but it is a mistake to assume that because we find such decisions difficult there is something 'wrong' with us. We shall say more about this in our discussion of Therapy.

It is worth noting that *reciprocity* is important in friendship: if the degree of involvement between friends is at a considerable variance the friendship is likely to wither, because – as we have seen in the Forster passage – the expectations we have of friendship are considerable and we are disappointed and hurt if our friends do not appear to be as concerned with us as we are with them. Working out when concern becomes intrusion and respect for privacy becomes indifference is an ongoing issue in one's friendships and can be negotiated only between the individuals concerned, which is no doubt what is meant by the saying that we need to keep friendships 'green'. However these matters are dealt with, a basis of honesty and trust would seem to be a precondition. We shall say some more about these two notions in a later section.

Love

Love is regarded by many as what indeed 'makes the world go round' but by some as disruptive and problematic, so what is there to say about this centrally important interpersonal relation which appears to take up so much of our attention? Let us return to our Venn diagram: we see that in the case of friendship the boundaries of our selfhood are partially dissolved or invaded or breached; we allow our friends 'limited access' to what we regard as most important about ourselves – our time, affection, confidences, actions – and we do this *because* they are our friends. Closeness to them is of value to us because we like them and trust them and find our lives enriched by our interaction with them. However, as we have observed, this involvement is only partial and not exclusive, that is, we do not expect to be the *only* friend of another, although we hope to be a particular or close friend in some cases – the importance attributed by schoolgirls to the status 'best friend' demonstrates that friendships sometimes verge on a desire for exclusivity, but however great the intensity of the friendship it is not quite the same as the intensity of the love relation, or if it is, then it should perhaps be called 'love'.

According to our diagram, love approaches or is identical with the unification of two individuals, obviously not physical unification, but that of the two personalities. At its most extreme, the two individuals are totally absorbed in one another to the exclusion of anyone else: they share their time, tastes, activities – they strive to be transparent to one another so that it is almost as if they are one person rather than two. Thus it is that in this interrelation the two selfhoods merge, which creates an experience of both maximum belonging and maximum vulnerability. Each can do the other irreparable harm if they so choose, because they are to all intents and purposes 'inside' the other. In the discussion of self-esteem in the previous chapter we saw how important this was to an individual's being able to function and if this is threatened, as it can seriously be by those who are close to us, the damage wrought is proportionately greater. Thus love is the most hazardous interrelation of all, because while it provides enormous life-enhancing possibilities, it also can be utterly destructive, and many such interrelations vacillate between the two much of the time.

Furthermore, in modern society its problematic nature is aggravated by the greater urge to operate towards the individuating end of the spectrum so that individuals are increasingly unwilling to sacrifice their individuality in favour of that of another, which means that love relations in which one individual subsumes their individuality permanently under that of the other are becoming increasingly rare. We are now aware that the rosy picture of lifelong devotion between two individuals has frequently involved one of them 'calling the shots' and the other falling in with this. Is this too cynical a view? I think not: merely a more accurate one, because if what is being argued in this book is correct, the uniqueness of individuals means that coincidence of their projects is necessarily short-lived, so that continuing to follow the same paths or trajectories for any length of time must involve something *other* than this, that individuals order their preferences in such a way as to pursue coincident pathways because of other considerations than that there is coincidence *simpliciter*.

Thus while individuals may be attracted to one another in the first place because of shared interests and tastes and values (though that quite frequently is *not* the reason, but rather physical/sexual attraction, as I shall discuss later), what is shared may not persist: there will be divergences, so that those involved need to decide what response to make to their changed situations, situations which have changed partly because of changes in the individuals themselves and partly in external factors. It is not cynical but correct to observe that the intensity and all-absorbing nature of the love relation changes over time, but this is not to say that it may not persist in some transmuted form, one in which the selfhood of those involved reasserts itself without rupturing the bonds between them. Once again this can be decided only by the individuals involved, but this is what needs to be recognised, that there are no general rules and that those who claim there are, are surely mistaken. Thus this puts the responsibility squarely where it belongs, on the self- and other-understanding of the individuals concerned. Rather than seeking to 'recapture' the intensity and exclusivity of the initial experience, attention must be given to the significance of the inevitable change-over-time, to realising the futility of 'trying to put the clock back' to remembered former bliss; as Robert Browning in 'Home-Thoughts, from Abroad', expresses it where he speaks of 'The first fine careless rapture'.

This discussion of love may seem a rather sombre characterisation of what for some, or even many, is for some of the time a source of ecstasy and delight. After all, much literature, music and visual art is concerned with love; but the emphasis is surely more on the travails of lost or unrequited love as in eg Schubert's 'Die Schone Mullerin', rather than a celebration of its more positive qualities.

One must be very careful in any theoretical discussion of love not to give the impression that it is all a matter of *reasoning*, rather than stressing the absolute centrality of *feeling* and *desiring*. Of all areas of human experience this is the one in which feeling and desiring are at their most intense and deep-seated – our surrender to another is a highly dangerous matter which can colour the whole of our lives for good or ill, and this should not be forgotten, or taken lightly. While we have been discussing what might be called romantic or passionate love, surely the most intense and deep-seated, other variants of the love-relation need some discussion because they share its features, although usually to a lesser extent. Furthermore, some of these can be a disguised version of the romantic love-relation and hence equally liberating or oppressive. The interaction between parents and children can come very close in intensity to romantic love (family *ties* can be seen as *attaching* the family members to one another but also possibly *inhibiting* them), as can that between friends; even loyalty to an institution, political party or one's country can take on the obsessive intensity of romantic love and give rise to the same problems, as we shall see when we come to discuss Joseph Roth's *The Spider's Web* in Part Three.

What we should recognise is that a given human experience which is as important as the other givens we have been analysing (embodied individuation etc) is our capacity to form *attachments* to other human individuals which can be of such strength that they structure everything about us. Aristophanes' fanciful characterisation, as given by Plato in *The Symposium*, to the effect that each of us is incomplete until we find our 'other half' makes this point very well. It is another example of the importance of belonging as an analgesic against existential loneliness, in this case the specific one of finding a 'mate', although the reproductive connotation of this term is not necessarily appropriate. Increasingly, as the number of same-gender partnerships shows, reproduction is regarded by many as less important than the closeness and warmth of another. Whatever the explanation, and I don't think there could be a conclusive one, we constantly seek to pair with another human being, and in spite of the hazards of doing so, consider ourselves 'incomplete' if we do not, as the Lonely Hearts columns of almost all magazines and newspapers (including, at least at one time, the *London Review of Books*) demonstrates, along with the phenomenon of computer dating.

What can we conclude, then, from our reflections on these four types of interpersonal relation – civility, acquaintance, friendship and love? We have seen that they form a progression from the most casual and undemanding interactions, that they are all variants of the belonging end of the spectrum or continuum, civility only distantly so – little is required of us in terms of giving up our own projects for another – friendship and love increasingly demanding our time, attention and concern, to the point, in the case of love, where we may lose (temporarily) all sense of our *own* self because it is as though it has unified or merged with that of another to create a compound being. But in all these types of interaction, we may need constantly to reassess their nature because they can change incessantly: acquaintances may become friends, friends may become enemies or lovers, lovers friends or enemies, and so on. The configurations are subject to constant change, although some may remain constant over many years. We may become neither more nor less friendly with our next door neighbour for twenty years; school-friends may remain lifelong friends, spouses grow old and grey together. In all cases, as we have observed, a fundamental precondition of interactions involving closeness and warmth is reciprocal *honesty* and *trust*, and we shall say some more about these two notions in a later section.

Physical / Sexual Attraction

So far we have been discussing what might be called Romantic Love in the context of the invasion and dissolving or at least perforation of boundaries.

However, something should be said about Physical/Sexual Attraction because for many or most human beings, apart from a few natural celibates, it is *very* strongly felt and a source of both ecstasy and despair, the latter sometimes leading to suicide or even murder.

Often taken to be synonymous with romantic love and certainly frequently intertwined with it, it can sometimes be quite separate from it in difficult-to-explain ways.

In Western society, the prohibitions and frustrations, largely stemming from religion, to do with previous moral views, have been replaced by an anything-goes attitude to sexual activity, partly, perhaps mainly, because of reliable contraception so that unwanted pregnancy is no longer as great a problem as it once was. The loosening of moral prohibitions has developed alongside this, in ways which are not necessarily straightforward.

While the root source of sexual attraction and activity may well be to perpetuate the species, it has been replaced for many by the notion of 'recreational sex' which carries little other than immediate satisfaction of desiring; certainly not implications of responsibility and loyalty.

However, sexual attraction's intimate connection with more serious notions of love persist and cause a good deal of confusion and heartache; hindering rather than helping individuals to understand their most strongly felt interpersonal relations. The removal or diminution of the reproductive imperative does little to assist same-sex individuals, attracted to one another, to work out how to live with one another. The question of boundaries and the threats to selfhood remain, compounded rather than lessened by strong physical/sexual attraction.

Still in the context of challenges to and possible erosion of selfhood, let us say something about a number of other features of human interaction. These are Cooperation and Competition, Honesty, Trust, Gratitude, Envy, Jealousy, Resentment and Paranoia.

Cooperation and Competition

At first sight this dichotomy may appear to correspond to the belonging/ individuating spectrum, such that Cooperation occurs between those wishing to belong, Competition between those wishing to individuate, but while there is some such correspondence it is not precisely the same. Indeed if one takes the essence of competition as being concerned with winning and losing, then to win is to separate oneself from others and to gain power over them, and to lose is to *be* separated from others and to lose power over them. Thus another correspondence now appears to be that between this dichotomy and those of agents and patients, or autonomy/heteronomy. Let us stay with the notion of *power* for the moment – if we succeed we gain in power, if we lose we lose power, but winning and losing, success and failure depend on a context in which activities are graded in some publicly acknowledged way so that one can be clear about who has won and who lost, otherwise one has a situation like the Caucus Race in Lewis Carroll's *Alice in Wonderland* where 'everyone has won so everyone must have prizes', as the Dodo says. This in turn depends on a grading of the activities in question in terms of their value or quality – some are valued more highly than others; and not everyone can have or achieve the most highly valued, because individuals' abilities *vary*. Thus, we can see that the notion of competition is presupposed by these graded values *and* by the assumption that only some individuals have access to the higher ones.

It can be argued that such pre-existing scales of values *create* the desirability of the goods or activities concerned – this is a constant criticism of Capitalism – and that individuals are encouraged to desire states of affairs which would otherwise have no attraction for them, and this is sometimes correct. However, whether or not this should be deplored or applauded depends on what the scale of values refers to, because some activities, Education for example, rely heavily on 'assessment' which, as well as the dubious feature of enabling us to judge others, also enables individuals to judge *themselves*, ie to know 'how they are getting on', and this is regarded as useful by those individuals. But is this 'competition'? It is certainly seen as such by those being assessed, in the sense that they constantly compare themselves with others and are elated or deflated according to where they stand in such comparisons. The person 'at the bottom of the class' will have poor self-esteem, those at the top will think well of themselves because, in part, they are thought well of by others. In this case, it is not that everybody cannot be top, merely that, as a matter of fact, only a few can be because of the inequalities of 'natural endowment' – some people 'just are' cleverer than others.

A lot of thought has been given to the unfortunate consequences of this – that many individuals will feel that they are failures, or not much good – and attempts have been made to disguise the more painful implications of assessment, none of which has been spectacularly successful. Taking away systems of assessment means that individuals have no idea what, if anything, they have achieved; tinkering with 'marking systems' merely causes confusion and leaves all those involved with the sense that the problem has merely been swept under the carpet. Probably the most promising approach to the problem is to extend the range of activities in which individuals may participate and be judged in the hope that 'everybody is good at something' if one could but find out what it is.

Now, the crucial issue for our discussion is the relevance of these considerations to the development of unique individual potential. So far we have seen that the usual understanding of competition involves individuals submitting themselves to judgement under some pre-existing scale of values, and using how they 'perform' to contribute to their self-estimate. If they do not do so, either because they fear the outcome, or distrust the scale of values, they will have no means of forming such a self-estimate. Or will they? One might think the world would be a better place without competition or assessment, but the fundamental point is that, like it or not, formally or informally, we assess ourselves and one another *the whole time*; it is another version of our praising and blaming ourselves and one another the entire time. Given the sophistication and complexity of human activity, itself the outcome of the incessantly *creative* sophistication and complexity of human self-consciousness, we constantly judge and assess what we do, and feel pleased and satisfied if we succeed or do well, and downcast if we fail or do badly. All human interaction, even at the most informal level, consists of our saying 'well done' or 'not so good, try again' to one another, from the most humble activity – mowing the lawn, boiling an egg – to the most elevated – writing a symphony, running the country. We could say that such assessments help us to understand the *meaning* of the activity; we place it in our own scale of values but we cannot do so without taking account of the public scale of values in which it features. Indeed we may question the public scale of values, either *vis-à-vis* other scales of values, or in terms of whether or not the activity should have any value, but this is not to get rid of such scales, merely to revise them.

Thus we can see that such assessment is intrinsic to the functioning of human consciousness, and that to wish to eliminate it is futile. What we can object to is the increasing tendency to translate assessment into *numerical* form, to make it quantitative rather than qualitative, because this is to create an artificial precision which bears little relation to the richness and complexity of human activity. This is a technique borrowed from the physical sciences where it has proved useful, but its value for understanding human experience is highly questionable; at its most absurd it treats human individuals as non-sentient physical entities, and encourages all manner of deplorable dehumanising tendencies in our treatment of one another. It is the far end of the spectrum in the move from the particular to the abstract and general, essential in acquiring understanding, but to be used very sparingly lest we lose sight of the essential particularity of human beings.

The relevance of these remarks to competition is that the urge to assess human individuals on some analogue of 'on a scale of one to ten' oversimplifies the diversity of human activity and has the disastrous effect of lowering the self-esteem of many individuals at the same time as *over-inflating* the self-esteem of some. How many individuals have spent large parts of their lives, even the whole of their lives, living a twilight existence because they 'were no good at school', or 'got a bad degree', or 'didn't get promoted', or 'were made redundant'? It may be thought that it is inevitable that there will be such casualties, in the light of what has just been said about the unavoidability of assessment, but some comfort may be derived from the realisation that the scales of values in terms of which we judge ourselves and others are constantly open to revision. They are not 'written in the stars', they are human constructs which have been formulated in an attempt to structure what is regarded as valuable by a given society at a given time, or rather, they have been formulated by a few individuals considered to be qualified to try and formalise what is regarded as valuable by a given society at a given time, or rather, again, regarded as valuable by a few members of a given society – ie those vocal and confident enough to have a view. Realising this means that, at least in principle, it is possible for individuals to suggest revisions to such scales, or additions to them, or even the elimination of some of them. What changes the 'in principle' to 'in fact' is that the individuals concerned make the effort to do so *and* that there is a willingness to listen to their suggestions.

Would this suggestion make any difference to the negative effect of 'failure' or merely spread the different ways in which one could fail? This surely will depend on how much importance the individual attributes to their position in the various scales of values in which they involve themselves, as well as how much importance *others* attribute to that position. If individuals 'measure' themselves *only* in terms of how they compare with others rather than in terms of the intrinsic worth of the activity for them, they increase the chances of being cast down by failure. In present day society we are surrounded by all manner of 'competitive' activities where individuals do measure themselves in this way – 'good qualifications', 'a good job', 'membership of the Golf Club', living in the posh end of the town, sending one's children to 'a good school', but thus it has always been (consider Molière's plays), although throughout history there have always been a few 'strong-minded' individuals who have rejected these 'determinants' and gone their own way.

If for 'strong-minded' one reads '*chez soi*', then we are approaching the issues discussed in this book. Only individuals who are at home with themselves stand any chance of distancing themselves from these enormously strong social pressures, not necessarily to reject all of them, but to assess them in terms of their appropriateness to themselves. But *that* is only possible if the individual has some *self*-understanding; only an individual who is clear about their own desires and purposes can decide to what extent social scales of values coincide with their own, rather than assuming that those values *are* their own. It requires a strenuous effort both to work out what the social scales of values are, and also to discover how far they suit our own often ill-defined desires and purposes. Of course it is almost impossible to completely separate the social valuation from the individual one – it takes a *very* strong-minded individual to persist in an activity regarded by others as abhorrent or stark raving mad, although there are some such, and it is unlikely that most of us will wish to engage in such extremes. Rather, if differences are not violently but subtly at variance with what is regarded as 'acceptable' it may not require that much decision and courage to pursue them, because they 'feel right' for the individual concerned.

We have mentioned 'intrinsic' worth as a possible alternative to 'social valuation' but this is not quite the right way to put the matter, because some activities may both have intrinsic worth for the individual *and* have a high social valuation; others may not, in which case the individual has to decide whether they should pursue the one or the other. It is not a simple case of 'always go for the intrinsically worthwhile' or 'always do what is socially approved' – this is another of those over-simplified dichotomies which seems attractive (because we have a *rule*) but is likely to get us into as much trouble as not having a rule. Rather, the choice is between following the one or the other *in the specific context*. We may wish most urgently to pursue our study of dragonflies to the exclusion of all else but *also* to join our partner in their setting up a business. Do we spend our time by the pond or in the shop? Setting up the business has a more obvious economic, public and social value; the study of dragonflies very little immediate value (except to the individual) and is likely to subject one to public opprobrium. Only an exhaustive analysis of the specific context will yield a solution – rules and maxims will offer only the crudest advice.

While there are possible advantages to competition in that, at least, it can enable the individual to keep track on 'how well they are doing' under some pre-existing scale of values, we should not lose sight of the *intrinsic* value of the activity in question. If the individual finds the activity 'intrinsically worthwhile, for its own sake', then perhaps it should be pursued regardless of whether or not it is valued by others. The study of dragonflies, though probably valued by other entomologists, may be considered without value by many others, and might need a very strong-minded individual to pursue it. As we have said, it is a matter of individual choice and organisation to decide the matter. It would seem preferable to keep a place for the pursuit of the intrinsically worthwhile, and not become totally enmeshed in winning and losing, as so much of modern life appears to involve.

Certainly, 'winning' may lead to making possible the pursuit of the intrinsically worthwhile, for example winning a monetary prize may enable the individual to have the freedom to pursue their own, otherwise unavailable, trajectory as a *means* to an *end*.

This is the point at which we should say something about *cooperation* because, as we observed at the beginning of the section, it appears, at first sight, to be the mode of being closest to the belonging end of our spectrum. If we 'work with' others rather than in competition with them, then while this increases the chances of completing the project in question, does it enhance the expression of unique individual potential? Once again, we need to look at specific contexts: in general, *if* individuals genuinely share the aim or purpose in question, it does aid the expression of individual potential, but this is only sometimes the case. As frequently, perhaps more frequently, we join others in their projects because of either our affection for them, or their power over us.

Thus we can only tell what the precise relations are in a cooperative situation by close analysis of it. Why does this matter? Surely if those concerned are pursuing some project successfully there is no need to ask too closely about the status of each individual's input? The point is that the convergence between the individuals' purposes, even if there is one, is likely to be short-lived because such convergences are unstable in principle. *Divergence*, expressing unique individuality, is a constant threat to them. If this is realised, individuals may pause before committing themselves to such cooperative enterprises, and either refuse to do so or, if they regard the project as worthwhile, *choose* to engage in auto-limitation in order to pursue it. But this will be *finite* auto-limitation – making open-ended or lifelong commitments are likely to end in tears although human experience is full of occasions which try to persuade individuals that they should make such commitments, from marriage to jobs-for-life (an increasingly rare phenomenon, however). (We shall mention oaths of allegiance later in this chapter, and also in the discussion of Joseph Roth's *The Spider's Web*.)

Of course one can see the attraction of the *security* of such states of affairs, because they enable individuals to feel that they can *depend* on others to act in predictable ways, and in a world full of unpredictable occurrences this is a comfort. But is the price to be paid too high? Once again we are talking about our belonging/individuating tension, and once again, there are no rules and no easy answers; one can only decide for each specific situation by reflecting on one's scale of preferences, the relative worth of the project in question, the implications of whatever choice one makes, and so on. Thus, it is an over-simplification to say that cooperation is good while independent action is bad; about the most one can say in general is that *willing* or *voluntary* cooperation is preferable to unwilling or grudging cooperation, not only because of the effect on the individual but also because of the effect of the unwilling co-operator on the others involved.

It may be objected that while this would be the ideal state of affairs, it is very unlikely that it could very often be realised – that would depend on a) those involved having thought through what they are doing and b) the activity concerned lending itself to being pursued only by those who genuinely subscribe to it. a) and b) are both pretty unlikely; life is much more of a muddle than that: the objection would continue, and this is of course correct. At present this is the situation on many occasions, but does this mean that one needs to give up under the difficulty? As with many other issues discussed in this book, a *climate* in which the desirability of certain stances and practices is accepted and made fundamental *can* have an effect eventually on how we interact with one another. It would be a mistake to claim that cooperation is a primary good without clarifying *how* it is achieved. We have seen the disastrous results of *imposed* 'cooperation' in the former Eastern Bloc where very few of those concerned recognised the claimed 'advantages' of a political system supposed to be based on universal cooperation. This is not to suggest that any other political system has been conspicuously superior but rather that any system which is not based on a careful thinking through of the 'goods' it claims to embody is quite likely to do more harm than good. The most important consideration in any discussion of competition and cooperation is the effect each has on the expression of unique individuality and of harmonious interpersonal relations, if it is accepted that these are the essence of worthwhile human experience. We have now seen that we need scales of values in order both to find meaning in our activities and to judge ourselves and others, but these need to be constantly interrogated and revised if they are not to have the effect of provoking a sense of artificiality and irrelevance about what we do, and indeed *must* be – because 'life moves on'. Insofar as appeal to scales of values is a feature of competition, and it is not the only one, then it may contribute to self- and other-understanding, but this is not to say that classifying human beings *only* in terms of 'winners' and 'losers' is desirable or necessary, particularly as such scales of values are not necessarily those of the individual concerned, nor are they immutable. Unfortunately, such scales have a profound effect on individuals' self-esteem, and taking them too seriously can make or break a human personality, encouraging excessive self-importance in 'winners' and a sense of excessive inadequacy in 'losers' (an example would be the effect of IQ tests). Whether or not this is an insoluble problem will depend on our views about the other issues which are under discussion in this book.

Cooperation, we have seen, can have the effect of enabling us to pursue projects we could not achieve individually, but whether or not so doing contributes to the expression of unique individuality depends on the willingness or otherwise of those involved to commit themselves to such projects. Whether or not there is any choice in the matter will, in turn, depend on the climate in which individuals operate.

We shall postpone reaching any final conclusions on these matters until we have said something about several other notions in interpersonal relations. Let us now turn to these:

Honesty   Trust   Gratitude

In our discussions of those relations which bind individuals to one another, themselves based on the affinity or 'sympathy' between humans – our ability to be affected by and respond to the experience of others – we have mentioned in passing that we have certain expectations of one another without which any 'contact' with one another would be problematic or impossible. The most important of these are Honesty and Trust: in the more distanced relations of civility we would prefer it if others did not mislead or betray us, although if they do we are not too devastated, but in friendship and love this requirement is very much stronger, so that if it is not met the outcome can indeed be disastrous. We have begun to see why this is so; it is because in these relations we allow the boundaries of our selfhood to be invaded or perforated and possibly *dissolved* by the other, and this means that we become vulnerable to them: they can do us harm. Thus we require that those to whom we stand in these close relations do *not* mislead or betray us, do not present themselves as other than they are, do not say things they do not mean, do not pass on our private confidences, do not give us a false estimation of themselves or of their view of us. And these requirements are reciprocal. Of course this is a question of how far they *know themselves* and what they are saying and doing – and the same goes for us.

But these requirements are *not* met a great deal of the time. Consequently our closest interpersonal relations are fraught with chronic difficulties which we have to see result from the belonging/individuating tension at its most intense. Does realising this merely clarify the issue without offering any way of resolving it? I suggest that clarification goes part way to resolution, because a central theme of this book is that *self*-understanding is a necessary if not a sufficient condition of structuring our lives to enhance the development of individual potential, ie to promote *flourishing*. If we realise that at least part of the reason why we find interacting with others so difficult is that it is of the nature of human nature to wish *both* to belong and to individuate, then what we may have achieved, at the very least, is the realisation that the problems thus generated *are* 'of the nature of things' rather than necessarily the result of individual deficiencies. And this, in turn, can have two outcomes: a) we can stop hoping for *general* solutions to our problems in terms of rules of conduct etc which will in some miraculous way make all the difficulties dissolve, and b) we can see that such difficulties can be resolved only in specific contexts as a result of their analysis by those involved.

One of the most persistent features of human beings is to assume or hope that *others* 'know better' and will solve their problems for them. This is why Kant's *What is Enlightenment?* statement is a central reference for this book. What we have been trying to show is that this is futile, and that every effort must be made strenuously to acquire one's *own* self-understanding: certainly with the advice and guidance of others much of the time, but only their advice and guidance rather than their dictation. Now, what has this to do with honesty and trust? We can see that if the self-understanding is a primary project of the individual which is itself a precondition for the formulation and pursuit of individual projects, then such self-understanding is in part acquired by listening to the views of others, most particularly those to whom one is close, ie who 'know one well', and these are individuals to whom one stands in friendship and love relations. If such individuals give one a false or misleading account this can lead to a false or misleading *self*-estimate, thus compounding the difficulties of one's interactions with others.

None of this is new; it is what human individuals have always done, although perhaps to less depth than is now the case, and appealing to models of the ideal person which are no longer fashionable or tenable. Consider how much Classical thought is devoted to discussing or showing the notion of 'honour', or how much 18th Century and 19th Century literature to trying to characterise 'gentlemanly behaviour', to take a couple of examples at random. The point is that human societies have always had notions of what makes an acceptable and decent person as opposed to a reprehensible one, and have placed individuals on a spectrum devised in this way. And in all cases, there is a requirement that 'acceptable' individuals (however defined) shall exhibit honesty, trust and loyalty towards at least *some* other individuals, although this may be quite a narrow section of their society. And this means *not* misleading and not betraying at least some others to whom they consider they stand in a special relation. It has always been thought that without this, human relations would disintegrate completely, and this is surely correct. No individual can operate at all if they trust no-one.

What, then, is the essence of honesty and trust? It is surely that individuals do their very best to act towards others in ways that can be *depended upon* – that they will, as far as possible, say what they mean and mean what they say; that they will not commit themselves to future courses of action unless they *intend* to try to carry them out; that they will not say or do anything to harm those who trust *them*; that, with at least some other individuals, they will do their best to promote their welfare and protect them from harm from others. These expectations are fundamental to harmonious interpersonal relations and, in spite of the myriad ways that individuals can mislead themselves and others, they can be fulfilled *sometimes* if the desire is there to do so. Unless at least some interpersonal relations have this feature, human existence would be entirely Hobbesian and intolerable: solitary, poor, nasty, brutish and short, as it says in *Leviathan*. One frequently hears it said that 'one can trust no-one', and, even more sadly, that one cannot trust those who are close to one – family and friends – and this may well be so for some people, but it is not clear that it *must* be so. Although we have been pointing out the difficulties made by the belonging/individuating tension, it does not seem to follow from this that relations of honesty and trust cannot exist between at least *some* individuals, but it does depend on the ability of *all* those involved to make a resolute effort to be as clear as possible about their own views and desires, for only if this is so can they express and communicate them to others.

Another cluster – of actions and attitudes arising from feeling-states, or possibly behavioural/emotional dispositions – which bind us even more firmly to others, but which nibble away at our autonomy, is:

Promising, Loyalty, Oaths of Allegiance

An adhesive which binds individuals to one another is the demand for and giving of *promises*, where individuals commit themselves to some future undertaking, a source of comfort to the promisee, a source of unease to the promiser, because their autonomy is threatened.

These dispositions produce a sense of security and reliability to the receiver *if* the promises, assurances of loyalty and so on are honoured... *if*! Assurances of loyalty on the part of the giver become increasingly serious (and punitive) at the social, legal and political level, where failure to honour what has been promised can have very serious consequences, including imprisonment and even death. At the interpersonal level, the most widespread is probably *marriage* vows, where promises of fidelity and so on *used* to be taken very seriously but are taken far less so nowadays. This 'loosening' of promised bonds is viewed by the stiff-necked moralist as 'a shocking decline in morals', but may equally be argued to be the result of an increased assertion of independence (autonomous following of unique trajectory) by the individuals involved. The jury is still out on this matter!

Gratitude

This is a peculiar binding relation between individuals which, significantly, is usually characterised in chilly monetary terminology – we have 'debts of gratitude', we 'owe' one another favours, we 'pay off' obligations, and so on. The underlying idea appears to be that if we do something 'for' another individual, then this binds them to do something for us 'in return'. If they do, then the debt is cancelled or 'paid'. Such actions are supererogatory ie beyond what we feel 'obliged' to do for others by family or professional requirements. The theory is that we do not expect to be thanked for feeding our children or doing our job – although in practice this is rarely so! – but if we do something over and above such obligations, then the recipient feels obliged to 'return the favour'. Thus, one could say that one creates a one-off obligation because one is not acting in accordance with some pre-established convention which demands of us that we should perform the act in question. This is to put the matter rather formally, and our actual experience is far more of a muddle than this, because most of us much of the time like, at least, to be thanked for what we do, even if it is only our job, and much of the time we like the thanks to be reinforced by some additional act.

Saintly individuals claim that they do not wish even to be thanked for what they do and this is reflected in much religious thinking. Consider Ignatius Loyola's prayer: 'To give and not to count the cost, to fight and not to heed the wounds, to toil and not to seek for rest, to labour and not to seek for any reward, save that of knowing that we do Thy Will.'

But note that although earthly thanks may not be required, what is required is the certainty that Thy Will is being done. While this may not be thanks, it is 'recognition' which is perhaps even more highly valued than mere thanks, especially when it is recognition by such a lofty being. The main point is that recognition of our efforts by others helps to boost our self-esteem, but this does not explain why it is that we feel obliged to do something in return for what has been done for us. I think the answer is that we do not like others to have *power* over us – we know, or assume, that the other *expects* some return; we are in their debt, and this is experienced as restrictive, in addition to the likelihood that the other will think badly of us. How often do people say 'after all I did for him/her!', which nicely sums up the situation. The genuinely pachydermatous seem blithely unaware of such debts of gratitude, but the more sensitive suffer agonies of indecision and doubt about receiving the bounty of others to the extent, in some cases, of refusing to allow anyone to do anything for them. Folk wisdom tells us that 'it is more blessed to give than to receive' and this is probably correct, but not for the reason normally assumed: it is easier to give than to receive because this causes others to be indebted to *us* rather than vice versa, and relieves us of the obligation to return the favour. Therefore it is more *difficult* to receive than to give.

As we have seen in our discussion of sympathy, it is extraordinarily difficult to 'get it right' when we attempt to help others, and we now have an additional problem which is that of burdening the other with a sense of indebtedness. If the 'help' has been inappropriate or unwanted in the first place, it merely compounds the discomfort or embarrassment of 'the helped'. Are there no circumstances under which we can do things for others without running into these sorts of problems? The answer would seem to be that they are probably very rare, perhaps only occurring between those who are very close to one another, but then we have seen that 'closeness' is a very unstable relation, prone to disintegration at any time, so that one cannot rely on the continuation of harmonious relations, and any divorce solicitor will confirm how vitriolic formerly close interpersonal relations can become when they do disintegrate. Those who have formerly 'shared everything' become extremely possessive and acrimonious about the most trivial things, drawing up lists of what belongs to whom and fighting every inch of the way to make their claims about everything from children and pets to the blue teapot. (An excellent film, *The War of the Roses* (dir Danny DeVito, 1989), portrays an extreme version of this.) After an extensive analysis of the fragility of human individuality we should be starting to see why this occurs, and how difficult it is to prevent.

The rather chilly analysis of gratitude in terms of the receiving and paying of debts may perhaps be modified by realising that not all gratitude is experienced or expressed in this way. Surely on *some* occasions, at least, it can be experienced as affectionate or even loving. The giver wishes to please the other, the receiver wishes to respond with equal pleasure – ie to 'return' the gift. Is there, in fact, an important difference between *cold* gratitude (incurring and paying a debt), and an affectionate/loving exchange (*warm* gratitude)? I would like to think so.

Envy, Jealousy, Resentment, Paranoia

So far, we have discussed those feeling-states in which individuals are *attracted* to one another. There is also a cluster of feeling-states which *distance* us from others, those of aversion or repulsion, at their most extreme, wariness in its milder forms.

The metaphor from Physics is surely illuminating.

We are both attracted to and repelled by others: they can be a source of comfort and security to us, but they can also hurt and damage us. On some occasions at least, we are wise to be wary or suspicious of them; they *can* indeed hurt or damage us. But, upon which occasions? This is an ongoing problem, partially resolved only by 'experience'.

However, in some cases, individuals become locked into a 'mind-set' of suspicions and grudges, whereby they become convinced that others possess belongings and lives which they would like to possess, or even consider that they have a *right* to possess.

All these feeling-states shade into one another: envy, the mildest; we would *like* to possess what others have, but do not feel we have any particular right to it. With jealousy, which can be violent and poisonous, we *do* feel we have a right to what another possesses; that we, not they, *should* possess it.

Resentment is more pervasive – a *generalised* grudge against others, the view that they possess what we should possess, that they have positions in some institution which we should have (or have had), and so on. This is frequently accompanied by unceasing jeremiads about 'the unfairness of life' (ie to them).

A fortiori, paranoia is an extreme version of resentment, involving the conviction that everybody is against them, and wishes them ill. It can be a diagnosable psychiatric condition, and individuals can become so deluded about themselves and others that any reasonable assessment of their interaction with others becomes impossible.

Resentment and Paranoia and the Disordered Individual

Just as one can adopt respectful, affectionate and loving relations with other individuals, one can also find oneself in relations of *aversion* to others. This can be more than merely 'disliking' certain individuals and avoiding them where possible, for we all do this. Rather, I am concerned with a more deep-seated trans-individual stance, that of *resentment*. Certainly we can feel resentment towards specific individuals, because we consider ourselves ill-used by them and this may well be justified, but it is also very common for individuals to feel this towards *all* other individuals, irrespective of whether or not they have done them any harm. How is this to be explained? Let us return to the general remarks we have made about the affinity between human individuals. We have seen that as feeling entities we are aware of and respond to the feeling-states of other humans but that this is not necessarily in terms of wishing to help them if they are suffering, or of sharing their elation if they are joyful – we may increase their suffering or seek to diminish their joy – but this is not necessarily because of our original sinfulness or nastiness; it depends on the specific context. Similarly with resentment: there may be situations in which our resentment is justified – the other has sought to harm one – but ascertaining whether or not this is so may be a difficult matter and we need to tease out the factors which contribute to such an assessment.

We have said that when individuals find the expression of their individual potential blocked or frustrated the experience is painful, and one of the ways of responding to this is to desire to cause pain in return to those whom one holds responsible. But it is this 'holding responsible' which causes the difficulty, because one needs to be clear about a) an accurate assessment of the situation, b) one's own role and responsibility, c) others' role(s) and responsibility, and there is likely to be considerable lack of clarity in some or all of these. Because of the importance of our own self-esteem, it is tempting to blame others or else impersonal forces beyond our control, rather than ourselves. Thus, in a situation where we find ourselves 'injured' or blocked, we prefer to blame someone or something other than ourselves, because otherwise that would be to admit our own inadequacy – a blow to our (always fragile) self-esteem. Consider how frequently recourse is made to upbringing, social position, genetic make-up etc to explain (away!) one's inadequacies. It is a small step from this understandable move to adopting a general stance of unfocused blaming as an explanation for all one's dissatisfactions about oneself and one's life. And this is encouraged by theories which argue for human helplessness in the face of forces of which we are unaware and certainly cannot control: beautifully encapsulated by Anthony Rudolf in his poem 'Catalogue Sonnet' (*European Hours*), which I will quote at the beginning of the Conclusion.

Now, what is at issue in the present context is the effect of resentment within interpersonal relations, and it is important to realise that this sense of unfocused resentment is very widespread and frequently has a poisonous effect on human interaction. Because it is unfocused, resentful individuals have a sour grudge-against-life stance towards others resulting in unjustified suspicion of others' motives and intentions, so that they are incapable of judging any situation with any accuracy. One might call such individuals 'disordered' in the sense that they are not *chez-soi*; this absence is attributed to others, for example blaming others for their problems, attributing malign intentions to them, and explaining the actions of others in the most uncharitable terms. At its most extreme, this is called *paranoia* and may well be a 'treatable' condition, but part of the line of argument of this book is that on many occasions to label individuals as 'mentally ill' or 'in need of treatment' may be mistaken because it could well lie within their own powers to resolve their own difficulties rather than 'seeking professional help'. We have seen that *all* individuals are subject to a whole range of tensions and conflicts because this is the raw material of human consciousness due to the fragility and vulnerability of being sensate entities, and *not* necessarily because there is 'something wrong with' them. Thus the 'disordered individual' is *not* one who isn't subject to these tensions and conflicts but rather one who refuses to *recognise* their inevitability: thus, individuals who allow themselves permanently to be subject to unresolved internal conflicts, and whose lives consequently consist of directionless drifting.

It may be asked why such directionless drifting should be eschewed, and the answer is that the essence of human consciousness, as is being argued, lies in its intrinsic purposiveness, the formulation and pursuit of individual purposes and the pursuit of human *flourishing* through the positing and consideration of *alternatives*; and then the inexorable logic of the matter is that individuals organise their lives in such a way as to at least *try* to achieve their individual purposes. If they do not, and continue as heteronomous patients buffeted by any and all forces acting on them, then inevitably the outcome will be dissatisfaction for that individual. Furthermore, as we observed in a previous section, they will waste the time and energy of more organised individuals and, in some cases, of public resources which could be better employed; for example, considerable media attention has been devoted to Munchhausen's Syndrome (and Munchhausen's-by-Proxy) where a significant number of individuals *invent* illness in order to receive attention and medical treatment to the extent of inflicting damage on themselves and their children. Not that this is a new phenomenon: some individuals have always used 'illness' to gain the attention and care of others, but while there may be something 'wrong' with them, it is with their personalities rather than their physical bodies, and may require a quite different remedy from a medical one.

In general then we can see resentment as an interpersonal stance which may on some occasions at least have no justification in terms of intended harm between individuals, but rather reflects the experience of a non-*chez soi* individual.

This can have a most corrosive effect not only on others but on the individual concerned. Examples are plentiful – the individual who has failed to be promoted, who has lost a lover to a rival, who has had a bad review, who has seen contemporaries being more successful than themselves etc, and those concerned may fume, brood and fester because their sense of self-worth has been diminished, and some sort of perverted satisfaction may be derived from inflicting damage on others, even if they are not those who were responsible (if there were any such) for the original deprivation. It is extraordinarily difficult to change the stance of a resentful individual who is determined to see everything and everybody in the most unfavourable light; once locked into a resentful stance, all states of affairs will be regarded with suspicion and mistrust, however innocent and well-meaning, so that those interacting with such individuals will be largely wasting their time if they try to change it. One can only hope that it may be possible to create a climate in which resentment is not allowed to get a grip, rather than trying to cure it when it is firmly in place.

Heaven is Other People?

The picture of human interaction we have been exploring appears to be one of such doom and gloom that we would be inclined to agree with Jean-Paul Sartre in his famous play *Huis clos* (*No Exit*) that 'hell is other people', but is this correct? Before proceeding, we should say something about occasions when things 'go right' rather than 'go wrong', because they do occur, perhaps far more frequently than self-congratulatory pessimists are willing to admit. It is fashionable to constantly draw attention to the unpleasant, painful and disastrous aspects of human experience, and to say little about its worthwhile and enjoyable features. Those who emphasise the latter are dismissed as naïve or simple-minded or 'unrealistic'. It cannot be denied that for some people much of human experience is unremittingly unpleasant, and is intermittently unpleasant for all of us. Nonetheless, if we did not find life enjoyable and worthwhile at least sometimes we would perhaps be less upset when it is not.

Certainly there are many avoidable ills as well as unavoidable ones and we decrease the chances of minimizing or eliminating the first if we decide pre-emptively that 'nothing can be done' or that 'what can't be cured must be endured' without *very* careful consideration of what it may be possible to 'cure'. In the present context, while our interaction with others is often difficult, it is surely not always so – we *can* enjoy the company of others, we can find them worthwhile and interesting, we can find acting with others more valuable than trying to act alone, and because we sometimes run into trouble with this, it does not mean that we should not continue to try to achieve harmonious relations with at least some others. It has been suggested that the civility-relation may be all that is necessary with most of the people we come in casual contact with, and refusing to become involved in the impossible demands of universal altruism as more than a matter of principle, ie replacing it with benevolence or tempered altruism, releases our energy and resources for concentrating on developing worthwhile relations with a small number of other individuals. This does not mean that we close our eyes to 'the problems of the world', but rather recognise that inter-relations of any depth can occur only between small numbers of individuals if they are not to deteriorate into meaningless and shallow surface contact. This is to acknowledge that human individuals have only finite energy which needs to be organised with the utmost care if it is not to be wasted pointlessly – allowed to trickle away into the sand.

The picture now emerging is of human individuals as subject to myriad demands both from their own desires and from other individuals, very few of which can be met. Thus it is imperative that if anything approaching a satisfactory life is to be achieved, each individual must try to seize control by organising and directing these demands; and this in turn involves selecting among them and ordering their own preferences in the light of their self-understanding of what is important to them. And this, as we constantly reiterate, can be achieved only as a result of a continuous effort, without which we relinquish any chance of forming satisfying relations with others. This is not to say that we should wish the whole of our time and effort to be taken up with interpersonal relations; some individuals are very happy 'with their own company' for much of the time, and most of us are content with it some of the time. With the exponential development of human consciousness, this could be increasingly the case since our ability to think and imagine and 'live inside our own heads' is a consequence of it. If we do this as a matter of choice rather than because we find others so difficult to deal with, there can be no objection to it.

We shall now move on to a discussion of Conversation, one of the ways in which we might begin to improve our interaction with others.

4

CONVERSATION
AND THE RECALIBRATED INDIVIDUAL

(1) CONVERSATION AND THERAPY

We have already mentioned in Chapter One that communicating is one of the activities of consciousness, and we shall now look at it in more detail in the context of the belonging/individuating tension underlying interpersonal relations.

Communicating is regarded as a valued essential feature of human experience, but can it be achieved in such a way as to retain the value and to avoid its possible distressing and disintegrative features which can be the result of loss of selfhood? This is the question we shall now discuss by looking at conversation in more detail.

Very roughly there are four types or strands of conversation, which I shall call Practical Conversation (PrC), Social Conversation (SoC), Serious Conversation 1 (SeC1) and Serious Conversation 2 (SeC2), and the essence of these lies in the *aims* of the activity. Even though they rarely occur in their pure form, but rather interpenetrate one another much of the time, nonetheless, although they may become confused with one another, one can usually identify the basic strands in any particular conversation.

Practical Conversation

Practical conversation has the aim of making decisions in order to achieve some practical purpose – how best to drive from London to Edinburgh, or grow dahlias, or bring up children – where those involved wish to reach a decision as to how to act. *Social conversation* is more fluid in its aims: at its most trivial it may be no more than what has delightfully been called 'delousing', ie those involved wish only to share some human warmth and togetherness (the metaphor coming from animal grooming, eg apes and monkeys). It may also involve the exchange of views and information – 'what have you been up to?', 'where are you going on your holiday?', 'did you hear what happened to Tom and Mary last week?', interspersed with (usually) very short-lived statements of opinion about more 'serious' matters – 'what the government ought to do is ... ' or 'young people are not as they were in *my* youth ...' – and brief analyses and judgments about books read, films and plays seen, football matches watched, according to the concerns of those participating. Social conversation can be the arena for a good deal of power-play, showing off, wit and entertainment, as well as malicious and vindictive character assassination, the latter often passing for 'wit'. What is almost certain is that very few of those involved will be attempting to speak carefully in the sense of trying to achieve genuine communication, partly because there is not usually any 'agenda' of 'topics to be discussed' and consequently no particular aim to be achieved.

This is not to disparage social conversation, except perhaps its more vitriolic aspects; it serves the useful purpose of enabling individuals to become acquainted with one another, albeit at a very superficial level, and to gain some insight into a range of views and opinions which they may not otherwise know about. It also serves the even more useful purpose of enabling individuals to identify others whom they may wish to 'know better', although this is not likely to be achieved in a social context where there is a constant threat of interruption and disruption, as anyone who has tried to pursue a meaningful conversation at a party will confirm! Assuming that 'meaningful conversation' is valued, how is it to be achieved?

Serious Conversation 1

The first requirement is surely that the *aim* of the interaction shall be recognised as that of pursuing the discussion of some topic (or series of topics) at some length and to some depth, and this type of conversation is already 'in place' in the more formal context of education, where this is (or should be) the primary aim of the seminar or tutorial. The problem with this is that the topics under discussion are not normally chosen by those involved because they form part of a syllabus which must be 'covered' whether or not they are of particular interest, or any interest at all, to the participants (including the lecturer!).

An unfortunate consequence of this type of conversation, based as it is on 'logical' argument, can be that it encourages more attention being given to the demolition of others' arguments than to offering positive alternatives. This is all too prevalent in academic life where it has the effect of deterring and deflating the attempts of the timid and reticent while inflating the self-importance and confidence of the deflater. The terms 'logic-chopping' and 'cut and thrust of argument' capture the brutal tone of such exchanges and they are to be deplored.

Nonetheless, at their best, such conversations can be valuable, and they form the model of my *Serious conversation 1.*

Serious Conversation 2

The main point is that if one's *aim* is to 'see what can be said about X' rather than to 'reach agreement', then this makes a difference to the way in which the conversation is conducted, because those involved will feel under no obligation either to a) convince others of their views, b) be convinced by others' views, or c) reach agreement. Instead, their primary aim will be to tease out the often subtle and elusive *differences* in their individual views, and to articulate them as clearly as possible in the presence of, and with the active encouragement of, sympathetic others.

In the light of what has already been said about unique individuality, the importance of an arena in which its expression can be developed should be starting to emerge; we have seen that individuals find it difficult to establish for themselves what their *own* views, values etc are, much less identify those of others with any accuracy, and if it is accepted, as has been argued, that doing so is of pre-eminent importance for a worthwhile existence, then making available opportunities for relaxed attempts to articulate such views and values is of equally pre-eminent importance. (*Writers* may do this in the absence of an interlocutor, however, they usually value 'input' from their readers.) This is not to say that *part* of such attempts may not result in agreement, of course they will, but that is not the *primary* aim. Human interaction is filled with half-stated, semi-articulated efforts to accomplish genuine communication where individuals try to talk to one another but are left with a sense of dissatisfaction and inconclusiveness which they often attribute to deficiencies within themselves rather than recognising that it is 'of the nature of things' that it shall be so.

Individuals who are attracted to one another understandably wish to 'get to know one another', but here the focus is on providing information about one another's lives and experiences, rather than on discussing what one might call 'a third term' ie the topic in question, where the experiences and interests of each will have a *background* relevance rather than a central one. In this way, SeC2 resembles academic discussion where, ideally, those involved are exploring some topic or issue in order to *understand* it for themselves, rather than exploring one anothers' personalities, although these will of course colour the contributions made. The diversity of opinions expressed will reflect the diversity of the contributors to some extent, except that in such situations there can be powerful pressures to discuss things in 'the accepted way' rather than express reservations or incomprehension for fear of being thought stupid or unnecessarily captious.

SeC2 on the other hand should contain no such impediments, for its main purpose is understood by the participants to be exactly this – to articulate reservations or incomprehension *in order to* clarify them, and to revise and restate any newly-arrived-at view and then explore it further. Thus such discussions are inevitably open-ended, because the pursuit of self-understanding is open-ended and intrinsically incomplete. All one can ever say is 'this is my view *now*' because there is always the chance that it will change in the light of new experience and new discussion and the *incessant creativity* of human consciousness.

SeC2 may also be thought of a type of *indirect* therapy where the focus is on the topic discussed rather than on the personal experiences of the participants.

Therapy

Why such opportunities are so important should become clear as our argument continues, but before attempting any summary of our conclusions we need to say something about the notion of 'Therapy' if only because it is a very fashionable term (and practice), and 'the talking cure' is sometimes used as a synonym. Thus we need to see in what ways it differs from 'conversation' as discussed in this section.

It is the general view that individuals who are upset, worried, distressed or, in general, not *chez soi,* benefit from talking about their problems to another, and this is surely correct in many instances. Externalising one's problems can diminish them and make them more manageable, so that what seemed insuperable becomes less so as a result both of trying to articulate them to oneself, and of hearing others' views of them.

A distinction might be made here between 'counselling' rather than 'therapy'. (Since the terminology surrounding the topic of therapy is so varied, it is necessary to resort to *stipulative* definitions ie those for the purposes of *this* discussion.) Counselling tends to be fairly short-term help with issues like bereavement, whereas therapy tends to be a more long-term process of treatment for people suffering from neuroses, lack of coping with various life issues, general depression, and possibly what we call 'disordered' thoughts/behaviour. Counselling typically involves talking-through and listening, therapy will also involve this to various extents, but will be guided by such things as dream interpretation, free association, archetypal analysis, etc., depending on the type of therapy involved. Some forms of psychotherapy can be close to counselling though not limited or even mainly involved with specific causes of psychological/emotional turmoil, such as grief, or goal-oriented in the sense of overcoming specific phobias etc, as with behavioural therapy, but aimed at recognising and dealing with more general psychological/emotional states and modes of behaviour and attitudes with the aim of achieving well-being. Solutions may present themselves which otherwise would not be available to the person concerned, and considerable relief may be obtained. If this is what is meant by 'therapy' that is fair enough, but what one may have doubts about is 'professionalising' or 'medicalising' this activity, because this tends to result in unhelpful thinking and practice to the effect that those concerned are 'ill', ie that there is 'something wrong with them' on a par with physical illness, so that all too easily the difficulties of human existence are viewed as diagnosable and curable in the same way that, say, ear-ache or indigestion are. Charles Taylor observes in *Sources of the Self* that over-medicalisation of society diminishes autonomy, and Ivan Illich has also written powerfully on this subject in *Limits to Medicine*.

Because the distinction, if there is one, between physical and 'mental'/psychological illness is a *very, very* grey area, hotly debated, it will be regarded as very contentious to suggest that this is not necessarily or always so – that grief, heartache, desperation, despair do not resemble physical illness all that closely, and that while it may be possible to 'get some pills for' all of these, this may not be the best way of alleviating them: that in fact remedies may lie in some quite different direction. Certainly the two most common ways of 'treating' these 'conditions' in modern society *are* either or both 'pills' or 'talking therapy', the latter conducted by a 'professional', but neither is spectacularly successful in 'curing' or even alleviating experiences which are surely an intrinsic part of human existence. (And what of those who are 'wired up' all wrong, ie have something wrong with their *brains*? – too large a topic to pursue here.) It should be said immediately that this is not to say that such experiences will inevitably 'consume' individuals for very large parts of their lives, only that in some circumstances they may be not only inevitable but also that we would not wish them to be eliminated from human experience; for example, we would regard it as 'unnatural' not to grieve for the loss of someone close to us, or not to be in despair at the failure of a treasured project, although if either the grief or despair in these cases persisted permanently we would consider that 'unnatural', because individuals do possess the capacity to recover from the most grievous experiences in 'normal' experience (though some choose to *abstain* from this). The question is, what is to be understood by these terms?

The question is whether we require *depth* in human experience in spite of all the implications of that, or whether we prefer to settle for superficiality and shallowness; for contentment rather than happiness or worth. *Prima facie* we might be inclined to opt for depth and worth, but with reflection and experience of 'the slings and arrows' this may involve, we may become disheartened and decide that only contentment is bearable, that the suffering and despair that may result from the pursuit of depth are intolerable. And many people do experience despair of such intensity that they choose to end their lives rather than remain conscious. We are told that this is increasingly the case in Western society, and all manner of psychological, sociological and political explanations are given of why this is so. Alternatively, and equally unsatisfactorily, unwilling or unable to contemplate the possible outcome of searching for worth and meaning, many others turn their backs on such attempts and settle for short-term satisfactions which require little effort and personal 'investment', and which, consequently, are not highly valued.

Yet others, for the same reasons, resort to 'flight' from the importunities of actual human existence and devote themselves to 'altered states of consciousness' brought about by drugs or religious experience, sometimes claiming that these bring about not just an alternative but a *superior* mode of experience, as we have briefly mentioned in the discussion of transience and transcendence. What is common to all these strategies is the recognition that human experience, as it is normally understood, can involve unacceptable levels of suffering, with the concomitant threat of the disintegration of selfhood. Thus for those who wish to avoid these dangers, and they are considerable, it is understandable that they should sacrifice the possible 'highs' in order to avoid the equally possible 'lows', but before seeing this as a source of regret and urging that one is only 'fully human' if one takes on the full gamut of 'what life throws at us', let us look a little further at the assumptions which underlie these avoidance decisions. In the first place we often work with faulty models of what constitutes an ideal human existence, assuming that what we should be aiming at is a 'balanced' life, one in which we keep going without feeling too much or feeling too little. Such terms as 'harmony' and 'equilibrium' occur in such models (see for example Aristotle's golden mean, also Damasio on homeostasis and Adam Smith on moderation), and those who are considered to match the model are regarded as 'well-adjusted', while those who fail to do so are 'ill-adjusted' or 'unbalanced' or 'unstable'. These terms are common coinage of everyday life; we constantly use them of ourselves and others to indicate approval or condemnation, to such an extent that they may assume the distanced status of 'labels' requiring no further reflection.

A further connotation of this model, appealing to the notion of 'balance', is that individuals should have 'wide-ranging' interests rather than just one or two, where the latter is often regarded as 'obsessive' or 'limited' rather than 'healthy'. Consider how many works of popular psychology recommend 'getting out and about, making new friends, taking up new hobbies or moving to a new area' as a way of alleviating unhappiness, and this may well have the required effect, but not necessarily; not necessarily in that it may not alleviate the suffering, or it could be that the unhappiness should be lived through rather than alleviated by artificial means. One can set against this those whose lives have been 'living hell', or certainly very unhappy, but who would not *themselves* have wished it otherwise because what they have done and learned has been of worth to themselves, however high was the price to pay. See for example the philosopher Ludwig Wittgenstein, who said: 'Tell them I've had a wonderful life', despite obvious psychological anguish. However, it is a commonplace to speak of 'tortured genius', and the term has considerable glamour, but it is worth remembering that while many geniuses have been tortured, many tortured people are not geniuses, and it could well be that the torture is not necessary or inevitable.

This, then, is another faulty model – the self-deception which may result from assuming that one's unhappiness is an indication of and natural accompaniment to one's remarkable talents. It is always difficult to ascertain to what extent the eccentric behaviour of those who are generally regarded as exceptionally gifted is consciously adopted by them, and to what extent it is a feature of which they are unaware because they are totally absorbed in what they are doing. One suspects that there is some element of the former in quite a few 'geniuses', especially when it can be used as a means of boosting their importance in the eyes of others, as well as getting out of mundane commitments and responsibilities. There are probably as many very talented people who look and behave like bank clerks as there are those who look extraordinary and lead rackety private lives. The importance of these considerations for our discussion is that 'models' can be dangerous, both if one fails to match them or if one does – it very much depends on how slavishly they are imitated. Slavish imitation must always be a mistake because no one individual resembles another enough for it not to distort the selfhood of the imitator, suppressing features which should be developed and encouraging those which might be better suppressed.

It is unavoidable that we look to others' lives for *some* assistance in organising our own, but we need to be very clear-sighted and cautious about it if we are to avoid assuming ill-fitting mantles rather than constructing ones which suit us better.

With these observations in mind, what can we now say about 'therapy'? We have already deplored that those who find their lives difficult resort too readily to the assumption that they are 'ill' and 'need professional help': these terms are very widely used today and my contention is that many people should not so classify themselves (or be classified by others), and that 'professional help', while it no doubt plays an essential role in present-day society, may not need to do so, or at least not such a pervasive one, in a different climate where self-help and interpersonal help might largely replace the 'professional' as at present conceived. But for that to occur, recognition of the fundamental features of human nature explored in this book would have to be a pre-condition, and there is a long, long way to go before it is achieved. At present, as Thomas Nagel says in *The View from Nowhere*, we have little or no idea how to live, how to treat one another or how to organise our societies. And the ferment and pandemonium of our present existence has the potential either to turn into triviality and irrelevance or to enable us to transform ourselves into beings capable of as yet undreamed of flourishing.

Undoubtedly human individuals desire above all to achieve purposes which are important to them, but they have enormous difficulty in both ascertaining what is important to them, and working out how to achieve it. When they fail in either or both of these ways, they become dispirited, because their desires are not only *felt* but are also the motors which enable them to continue to live. We have seen that frustrated or blocked desires are experienced as the source of much human suffering, and that the more complex and long-term the desire and its concomitant purpose (or sets of desires and purposes), the more intense and deep-seated the suffering. But, the satisfaction of such desires and purposes can bring equally deep-seated and intense joy and sense of worth. Given that it is of the nature of human consciousness constantly to generate new and ever more complex purposes, it is scarcely surprising that there will always be a danger of suffering from 'overload', even if we organise our responses to this spontaneous generation so as to 'channel' it in a way suited to our unique individuality. And this in turn requires a very strong sense of selfhood and *chez soi*, rather than the loss of self recommended in some religious thinking, or flight from actual human existence which throws out the baby with the bathwater. Only those individuals who are *chez soi* in the way we have discussed stand any hope of benefiting from these constantly unfolding possibilities.

Putting together what has been said about conversation and therapy, my suggestion is that a beginning can be made in the search for self-understanding by engaging in what we have called SeC2, where those involved endeavour to express their unique views and responses to the topic in question, whatever that may be; where the emphasis is on identifying unique *differences* rather than *similarities*, with the aim of externalising the *diversity* of aspects under which the topic can be considered. There will undoubtedly be such diversity: no two individuals will regard anything in *exactly* the same way, but occasions for realising this, much less articulating it, are rare unless they are actively created and encouraged.

What must be borne in mind for this to stand any chance of success is that a) human existence is complex, precarious and difficult because b) our desiring and feeling are an intrinsic part of our makeup, but c) at the same time so are reasoning, imagining, willing and communicating, so that d) human consciousness is constantly creating new configurations which it attempts to understand and use as a basis for action by e) the formulation and pursuit of purposes, many of which f) are in tension if not conflict with those of other individuals, but some of which may be shared with others, and g) a sense of worth and value is experienced by those who are *chez soi*, ie who feel that they are pursuing their own purposes rather than being obliged to follow those of others, but h) because of the loneliness of the individuated state, humans wish to belong with others at the same time as finding such belonging oppressive on many occasions because of i) their unique individuality (*alterity*) which means that their purposes can never be *identical* with those of others.

Given the stupefying complexity of human consciousness and hence of human experience, it is scarcely surprising that many individuals find their lives worthless or painful in the extreme, and are tempted to attribute this to their own failure, assuming that others can and do 'succeed' and hence must possess skills and talents that they lack. Consequently, if they act at all to try to remedy this, they seek help from those whom they assume 'know better', abdicating responsibility for solving their own problems and assuming the status of 'patients', frequently in the medical sense of the term. While it cannot be denied that *some* individuals are so severely not *chez soi* that professional help is necessary, many others are not and do not. We have suggested that a means of establishing whether or not this is so may be SeC2, where individuals converse with each other in a climate of trust and openness, and may well achieve the self-understanding necessary for continuing a worthwhile existence, but supposing no such context is available? In this case, recourse to 'professional' assistance is inevitable, and not necessarily entirely regrettable, because its great advantage is its comparative 'impersonality'. While a great deal can be achieved through conversation with one close to us, this perhaps requires that those involved be relatively relaxed with one another; if one or both are upset or desperate it is likely to generate more heat than light. Thus, there is a place for the 'uninvolved' who do not stand in any interpersonal relation with the upset individual, so that they can comment on what they are told without being held to account about it afterwards. (This may also be so with Arbitration in political and industrial disputes.) It is often the case that those who are upset are unwilling to reveal their difficulties to another, and if they do, subsequently to regret having done so since they have revealed their weakness and articulated matters they would prefer to remain private. This is the rationale of the notion of 'the confessional', and its secular equivalent, organisations such as The Samaritans where anonymity is guaranteed by the use only of first names. A more informal version of the same is that of talking to a stranger on a train – one avoids the embarrassment of having to meet the person again.

What, then, may be concluded from the lengthy analyses of this chapter? We began by noting the tension between the desire to belong and the desire to individuate which is the result of our embodied, already individuated, feeling natures, and which cannot be changed radically without unacceptable distortion of the potential of human consciousness. We can suppress desiring and feeling and give pre-eminence to reasoning, we can eschew reasoning and 'follow' our desires and feelings without 'taking thought', we can engage in flight from the importunities and difficulties of actual existence by ignoring them as far as possible in favour of exploring imagined worlds or religious notions of 'eternity' or '*nirvana*' which are not subject to the change and dissolution of the actual world.

(2) *THE RECALIBRATED INDIVIDUAL*

It is evident that we are at a primitive stage of moral development. Even the most civilised human beings have only a haphazard understanding of how to live, how to treat others, how to organise their societies.
                                            – Thomas Nagel, *The View from Nowhere*, OUP, 1986, p186

My starting point is to agree with Nagel's statement quoted above – although he wrote this over thirty years ago, little seems to have changed – that we are at a primitive stage of moral development, and that almost everything is left to be done, although it must be built on what has been achieved so far rather than overturning it and beginning again, even if such a thing were possible. Such radical attempts have almost always ended in tears, creating more problems than they solve, eg the French, Russian and Maoist Revolutions, so that we do well to move cautiously.

I have characterised the human individual as a unique entity, unique not only in terms of spatio-temporal location but also in terms of their physical and *psychological* make-up. And human individuals are *furthermore* the site or locus of the dynamic system of *consciousness*, which means that they act purposively, remember the past, anticipate the future, consider possible non-actual states of affairs, and are aware that they do so: they formulate goals and purposes, act to achieve them, and reflect on what is done. And because of each individual's uniqueness the purposes of one will not coincide with those of others, or at least not completely so, although this may not be clear to them partly because individuals find it difficult to articulate to themselves and to others precisely what their purposes are, partly because our affinity with other humans encourages them to go along with the aims and practices of others for fear of incurring their disapproval or animosity or worse, or merely because it is easier.

Human individuals are embodied rather than free-floating consciousnesses, so that their experience is fundamentally that of an entity capable of *feeling* through sensation both pleasure and pain, and a dozen complex analogues of these. This is crucially important in trying to understand what it is to be human because, in analysing the undoubtedly dizzying achievements of higher levels of consciousness, the extent to which these are grounded in feeling and desiring is often overlooked, or put quietly aside because it so difficult to talk about philosophically. Nonetheless, feeling/desiring underlies everything we do and the choices we make about what to do next are both determined by and assessed in terms of 'how we feel about' them. This may be disguised by saying that we choose to do what we do according to eg whether or not there are good arguments in favour of it, or whether or not it seems morally right, but at bottom, if we ask *why* we find the argument 'good' or the morality 'right', the answer is that we 'like' it, not in the trivial sense in which we like cream buns, but in the more serious sense of our 'approving' of it. And why do we approve of it? Because it matches with our deeply but intuitively felt sense of self. This is not to deny that there may not be a great deal of intermediate argument, consultation of the views of others etc before we reach this conclusion, but *ultimately* the test is whether or not it *feels* right to one. Or should be. Much of the time we go along with the views of others because we are unclear about our own views but, since life goes on, decisions have to be made and actions performed whether or not we are convinced about their 'rightness'.

Do the discussions of this book offer any illumination of this problem? Only this, that *perhaps* if individuals see the importance of trying to achieve self-understanding, and of interacting with others on a basis of respect for alterity, then the problem will be minimised, although never eliminated. Perhaps there will be greater tolerance of one another's mistakes because the difficulty of the task is appreciated; perhaps slowly, *very slowly*, as more and more individuals contribute their own articulations of their own individuality, a clearer picture may emerge of how human individuals might, could and should live. We are now at a point in human history when at least some of the former threats to human life have been eliminated or at least tamed so that for large numbers of people (but far from *all*) life is more than subsistence living; that is, we are *free from* a good deal but still unclear about what we are *free to* do: a distinction made by Isaiah Berlin in *Two Concepts of Liberty*. It would be a great pity if so much attention is devoted to the first that little thought is given to the latter.

It would be a great pity if humanity were moving into the type of situation foreseen by H.G. Wells in *The Time Machine*, where all the necessary work is done by the Morlocks underground (in present-day society their role is taken by science and technology and automation) while those freed from the drudgery, the Eloi, drift about aimlessly above ground.

One of the more encouraging features of modern life is human concern for others, for non-human animals and for the planet in general ... Individuals should take thought about their fellow humans, and not just from an enlightened self-interest point of view. I think it is a mistake to leave out a crucial component in moving towards this. In my view individuals must put their own houses in order as well as attempting to legislate for others, and this is what I have been urging in this book. Surely it is only when one is actively exploring one's own potential as fully as possible – and this must be done through interaction with others (see Chapter Three) – that one is in a position to decide *what* overall aims would be desirable for humans as a whole. It needs a far fuller use of imagination and sympathy than we have at present to fully appreciate the total unacceptability of *any* humans at all being the victims of avoidable suffering. It needs equally an exercise of imagination and sympathy to realise the extent of human diversity, and following from that, strenuous exercise of reason to work out ways of accommodating and developing this diversity.

As Nagel says, we have only the most haphazard understanding of any of these matters, so that we are scarcely in a position to formulate grand plans for the whole of humanity. Only when we understand ourselves a little better can we make tentative suggestions as to how our societies might be organised. This brings me to a reiteration of what I mean by understanding ourselves. I have adapted the term 'recalibrated individual' from John D. Crook's use of a similar one – he talks of the 'recalibrated ego' – in *The Evolution of Human Consciousness*. His approach to where humans should go next differs from mine in that he recommends a withdrawal from the importunities of the here and now in line with the practices of Tibetan Buddhism. This is an appealing option, and one which may well form *part* of everybody's experience, but not, I think, the whole of it, or only the whole of it for some people, because, for me, it downgrades the individual too much, failing to provide an opportunity for the development of individual potential and abdicating responsibility for the pressing problems of our current mode of existence. Nietzsche opined that Buddhism is the religion of a culture grown old and tired. Crook seems to want to bypass what, for me, is a necessary component of human practice without which we may not get to our endpoints, worthwhile as they may be, eventually.

The personal and particular is eschewed in favour of 'transcending' the individual, and this is 'a waste of consciousness' as Nagel observes in *The View from Nowhere*. Because individual experience is sometimes painful or worthless and selfish does not seem to me a good reason for rejecting it; I prefer to argue that it *is* possible to make it enjoyable and worthwhile and other-regarding. Surely many would agree that individual experience *can* be immensely satisfying; because this is so difficult to achieve does not seem to be a good reason for eliminating it as far as possible in favour of some universal '*nirvana*'. Nagel has put the matter very well:

> ... apparently it is possible for some individuals to achieve this withering away of the ego, so that personal life continues only as a vehicle for the transcendent self not as an end in itself ... this seems to me a high price to pay for spiritual harmony. The amputation of so much of oneself to secure the unequivocal affirmation of the rest seems *a waste of consciousness*. I would rather lead an absurd life engaged in the *particular* than a seamless transcendental life immersed in the universal.
>
> – *The View from Nowhere*, p219 – my italics

Thus one could see these approaches as therapeutic, as ways of dealing with the intolerable strain and discomfort of the individuated state so graphically described by Schopenhauer – one takes flight into the universal where things are less uncomfortable, leaving behind the pains and problems of the particular. I suppose my own approach could equally be called therapeutic, except that I am dealing with the cause rather than the symptoms, identifying frustrated or undeveloped potential as a remediable ill. *Properly managed,* the individuated state can be a source of worth and delight, one which differs qualitatively from the satisfactions of a more distanced mode of existence, where there is always the danger that one will tip over into *not caring at all* about human existence, one's own or anyone else's. This may be all very well if one has a firm belief in an afterlife beyond 'this vale of tears', but is indeed 'a waste of consciousness' if one has no such belief, and considers our present existence to be all we are going to have. In addition, how can one hope to understand and plan for the whole of humankind if one does not understand oneself?

This is not to claim that *all* suffering, disappointment, anguish, failure and frustrated hopes will be eliminated. Of course not, but perhaps they will be less insupportable than they are at present if only because the crasser forms of cruelty, brutality and indifference will wither away, and there is a more universal commitment to the importance of human *flourishing* and the minimisation of waste.

Perhaps there could be a paradigm shift (to borrow a term from Thomas Kuhn's *The Structure of Scientific Revolutions*) where the *recalibrated individual* is one who regards it as a primary good that unique individual potential shall be allowed expression, and this involves acceptance of a number of subsidiary claims:

1) that individuals shall be *autonomous agents* fundamentally, accepting heteronomous agency only by choice;

2) that autonomous agency can only be based on an active pursuit of self-understanding, since only when individuals have clarified for themselves what their unique goals are, are they in a position to act autonomously;

3) that self-understanding can only be achieved through interaction with others, where the aim is to articulate ways in which individuals *differ* from one another, as well as ways in which they resemble one another;

4) that 2) and 3) can only occur in a context of *respect for alterity*, ie for difference, and in a climate of benevolence;

5) that the obstruction and frustration of human purposes produces *disordered* individuals motivated by resentment, hatred and anti-human responses in general;

6) that the construction of any social organisation suited to such

recalibrated individuals can be done *only* by those individuals, ie those who have clarified for themselves, through discussion with others, *what* type of organisation would suit them best – to maximise the development of human potential. *While it is impossible at present to envisage what type of society this would be, we know that to impose blueprints from above on unreconstructed individuals is disastrous.*

7)   A very small beginning for this process might be through what I call 'serious conversation', whose primary aim *is* to articulate and explore unique individuality, rather than to reach agreement or win arguments, or 'get the better of' others (sometimes its main function at present). The crucial component of this is respect for alterity.

8)   Human consciousness is perpetually *creative*, and increasingly sophisticated, so there is no good reason why such constant recalibration of the individual should not take place if humans refuse to accept that they are powerless to intervene in and redirect their own affairs, or that the process is likely to be so difficult and painful that flight is the only response.

This account may give the impression that the recalibrated individual is condemned to an existence of a different type of unremitting toil from the one we are starting to leave behind, but of unremitting toil nonetheless. Formerly the toil involved was largely physical, the struggle to overcome the 'forces of nature' in order to survive; the recalibrated individual seems to be required to engage in a great deal of mental or intellectual activity, rooted in feeling, desiring and imagining, in order to overcome or at least keep pace with the forces of *human* nature which are constantly threatening to overwhelm and extinguish the individual. Is this an over-dramatic account? I think not, because, while it is perfectly possible to avoid or withdraw from such threats of psychological extinction by eg 'doing what one is told', this itself is arguably a form of psychological suicide.

But this is surely too gloomy a picture; much could be achieved through some adjustment in our view of ourselves, and of our potential.

It is understandable but not justifiable to:

a)   respond to the difficulties of human existence by *flight* eg postulating an after-life on which we should fix our gaze and ignore the here and now;

b)   ignore feeling and imagination because they appear to get in the way of solving immediate and pressing problems, as well as encouraging individuals to become self-absorbed;

c) employ draconian measures in order to force individuals into some common mould so that the projects of the few can be pursued with a minimum of disruption;

d) suppress the expression of individuality both because of c) and because individuals themselves find it difficult.

My suggestion is that the recalibrated individual is one who accepts that, if human flourishing is to be desired and encouraged, the *development* rather than the *suppression* of self-understanding (alongside other-understanding) *in order to* contribute meaningfully to social/political organization must be a *precondition* of co-operative enterprises with others and the formulation of social/political structures for organising human society. Only in this way, can the incessant creativity of human consciousness have an opportunity for expression in *uniquely* differing ways. Thus, unique creativity of consciousness can feed into and enrich the myriad *possibilities* available to it, or, in some cases, become *actual* in an informed rather than random and haphazard way.

PART THREE
LITERATURE

INTRODUCTION TO PART THREE
The Importance of Literature

IT WOULD BE DIFFICULT TO EXAGGERATE THE contribution which Literature makes to our understanding of human nature and experience. We are surrounded by books, plays, films ... which present us with Possible Non-Actual Worlds, resembling but not identical with the Actual World, but forming a penumbra (or many penumbras) of possible states of affairs and events in terms of which we attempt to understand our *actual* existence.

As the product of, and appealing to, *imagining*, Fiction is regarded with some suspicion, and sometimes rejected in favour of 'fact' as *the* correct account of human nature and experience. However, as has been pointed out in Part One, even our attention to the *actual* world is interwoven with imagining, as we attempt to make sense of the actual world's subject matter.

While other attempts to understand human consciousness by the Physical and Social Sciences have their contribution to make, they lack the immediacy and particularity of Literature where the reader is offered possible non-actual individual states-of-affairs and events resembling those of the Actual World, but, because of their different ontological status, they are in timeless suspension, rather than in the time-filled, transient precipitation of the Actual World. We can revisit them again and again because they *are* in timeless suspension, although they contain their own internal temporality, thus providing analogues to our Actual World experience. We feed insights from such works into enriching, widening and deepening our understanding of our Actual World experience.

In fiction, in particular, and possibly narrative poetry, we are presented with individuals working out the problems of selfhood and interpersonal interaction; charted in some detail, these portrayals are available for perpetual consideration by the reader, for comparisons and contrasts to manifest themselves, and to be fed into the formulation of future purposes and plans where they seem appropriate.

Discussions of Literature over the past fifty years or so range from time-honoured Liberal Humanism to the wilder shores of Post-structuralism and Deconstruction, the latter for some creating more heat than light and for others yielding some illumination and insight. The approach in this book is to focus on the philosophical questions discussed in Parts One and Two and to suggest ways in which they feature in the literary works discussed. Readers wanting to explore alternative approaches can do no better for an introduction than consult Peter Barry's books *Beginning Theory* and *Reading Poetry* – and there is a rich literature in these areas.

These preliminary observations form the background to my discussions of individual works of Literature, both Fiction and Poetry.

While poetry, normally more condensed than works of fiction, can also be said to present us with PNAWs, here, perhaps, there is often greater attention to the *particulars* of both language and experience. The condensed nature of most poetry enables both the poet and the reader to attend to certain features of an entity, an event, a state of affairs to the exclusion of myriad others to which attention could have been drawn.

There is an incessant interplay between the general and the particular in our experience and our understanding of it, the tension between searching for and attending to the one rather than the other being a crucial feature of the activities of consciousness. As Nietzsche has pointed out in his examination of the '*Origin of the logical*' (in *The Gay Science*, Book Three), we *need* to generalize (search for shared features in order to classify the subject-matter of the world), so that we can understand our experience, but by so doing, we may lose an appreciation of unique particularity. Kant, in the *Critique of Aesthetic Judgement*, has tellingly made the same point in his discussion of the aesthetic as the harmonious interplay of imagination and understanding *without* the formation of a *concept* (ie shared features). To 'get about', to negotiate our way through the world of 'lived experience' (the Actual World), we may and perhaps must ignore the uniquely particular. Thus, we would miss much that *is* uniquely particular were it not for our ability to 'switch' into reflective mode from the practical ('getting about') mode.

Psychologists have pointed out the importance of 'attention' – we cannot *attend* to *all* the subject matter 'bombarding' us, only to some of it. Hence, the switching to and fro between attending to the general, and to the particular. The person lost in contemplation of a tree or a landscape, may be attacked by a lion or a crocodile if she/he doesn't keep her/his wits about her/him – depending on the situation and location, of course.

Speaking of *attention*, one dimension of human experience to which we do not normally pay that much attention, is *sound*, so vision-based are we, although, as with vision, we are constantly bombarded with sounds, but secondarily to visual stimuli. With the exception of musicians and those who choose to attend to sound rather than sight, our primary navigational focus is on what we *see*, supplemented indeed by what we hear. Many people who live in urban settings long for 'the peace and quiet' of the countryside to escape the information anxiety of city life. But the 'peace and quiet' may be difficult to find! Editing out and enjoying the sound of birdsong, the wind in the trees, the ripple of water, may be obstructed by the sound of tractors, combines, clay-pigeon shooting and other country 'sports', off-road motoring, and the distant rumble of a motorway.

Poetry can invite us to attend to sound in two ways: it can have sound as its subject matter, and it can contain sound within itself (eg alliteration, onomatopoeia, rhyme and rhythm). The latter may be seen as part of a 'patterning' or perhaps 'structuring' process whereby not just sounds, but also images, individual words and phrases, etc, are organised throughout the poem in a telling way. Juxtaposition, fragmentation. ellipsis and fractured syntax are other features of some poems, employed variously and to various ends.

Let us return now to the issue of *particularity*. It is sometimes claimed or at least suggested that poetry *par excellence* 'captures the essence' of some state of affairs or event because of its brevity and sharpness. Accompanying 'clutter' of the subject matter is discarded or ignored in favour of 'going to the heart of things'. This may well be so – the reader may feel that they are encountering 'what oft was thought but ne'er so well expressed'. It may well be so that those who take the time and have the talent *do* express startling, searching locutions which seem to be 'the essence' of the subject matter. Nonetheless, given the incessant welling up of the creativity of consciousness plus the unique particularity of each individual there can be no end *to* such creativity – there are as many essences as there are experiencing individuals; although many of them may remain 'mute inglorious Miltons' (Gray's 'Elegy in a Country Churchyard'), at least some, perhaps with encouragement, can make their own innovative contribution.

The use of metaphor and simile is often cited as a central feature of poetry and there have been many academic analyses of them (eg Max Black, *Models and Metaphors: Studies in Language and Philosophy*; Paul Ricoeur, *The Rule of Metaphor: The Creation of Meaning in Language*; Michael Polanyi and Harry Prosch, *Meaning*). Certainly the bringing together of the otherwise disparate features of entities, states of affairs and events can surprise and illuminate one's view of them, but such conjunctions may have only a limited 'shelf-life' before they deteriorate into clichés (eg 'Man is a wolf to man') or become objectionable (eg 'The poor are the Negroes of Europe'), or become absurdly strained, as Ogden Nash's satirical poem 'Very Like a Whale' (widely available online) demonstrates.

We could also say that these various poetic means enable the poet to reveal things *as* vivid through vivid language; or bring to light what might otherwise be hidden, in as much as:

> [we need to refer to] the desire to explore modes of thought, feeling and imagination, within or in terms of the possibilities of a material medium, and to discover and disclose aspects of existence and experience – beyond the merely familiar and conventional.
>
> – David Miller, *Art and Disclosure*, Stride Publications, 1998, p16

At this point, we can see the coming together of what has been said in Part Two about SeC2 *conversation*. In both cases, there is an opportunity for individuals to try to articulate their own unique point of view, in an interpersonal context with SeC2, and in an (initially) private context in the case of the poet.

What may be considered by the reader to be insignificant marginalia may be transformed into an essence by the poet who, as it were, shines a spotlight on some hitherto ignored aspect of the subject matter or event. Dependent on the skill of the poet, *that* aspect might be seen as *the* essence of the matter. It becomes *memorable*.

We may ask how these general remarks about poetry relate to the central concern of this book, ie the relationship between the Actual and the Possible Non-Actual. We have discussed the interaction between our *actual* sensory experience, and our imagined experience of the non-actual, usually in terms of 'worlds', but perhaps in the case of poetry, because of its often condensed brevity, we should talk of segments, slices, shards or slivers of worlds, in as much as *certain features* are brought to our attention.

We have already referred to *aspects* of states of affairs and events often being the focus of poetry, and suggested that this relative brevity enables us to consider *that* aspect to the exclusion of others. However, this may mean that what *is* said causes *resonances* with other associated subject matter, unstated but available to consciousness by their associations for the reader.

The approach of Part Three, which these general remarks indicate, is to show how the metaphysical issues embedded in consciousness (discussed in Parts One and Two) can illuminate our understanding of works of literature and their relevance to experience-in-general. Thus I provide only brief synopses of the works in question in order to give prominence to the metaphysics.

5

FICTION

May Sinclair, *The Life and Death of Harriett Frean*

MAY SINCLAIR'S *THE LIFE AND DEATH of Harriett Frean* (1922) provides an excellent example of the misunderstanding and misapplication of sympathy and altruism discussed in Part Two Chapter Three.

From early childhood, the protagonist, Harriett Frean, is encouraged to 'think of others' rather than of herself. She never emerges from the domination of her parents' values and dies a disappointed and unfulfilled old woman, reverting, as she dies, to the nursery of her first memories.

Self-sacrifice, without any real interest in or concern for others, has been the guiding principle of her life, and she has no notion of self-*worth*, of carving out her *own* trajectory. Not surprisingly, she is rarely happy. She gives up any chance of married happiness in favour of her friend Priscilla, because she thinks Priscilla wants Robin and that she, Harriett, should not 'put herself first' and try to have Robin for herself. She has no solid autonomous core from which to operate.

Is this because she is 'a woman of her times', times when self-sacrifice was widely held to be a virtue in women? Not necessarily, because there were some 'intrepid' women who did carve out their own 'pathways' in spite of widespread male domination of affairs, though they were certainly the exception rather than the rule.

Let us look in more detail at the story of Harriett's life: she is born into a comfortable, though ultimately precarious middle class existence, and her parents, locked into their own narrow moral principles, persuade Harriett to give up a favourite doll to another child, and to let a different child 'go first' at a party. She is never punished by her parents for misdemeanours, but told she will disappoint them if she does not 'act beautifully' (ie selflessly).

Harriett has a completely uncritical attitude to her parents, although her father later turns out not to be as distinguished as she had assumed, and also has been responsible for the financial downfall of another.

Her mother, who is in the shadow of her husband, practises the self-sacrifice both parents espouse and refuses to spend money on an operation which might have saved her life, or at least extended it.

The family servant, Maggie, is a very different person. Not much sympathy is shown towards her when she has a baby, in fact, Harriett sends her away because she finds the baby tiresome, but when the baby dies, Maggie returns and devotedly cares for Harriett because, she says, she likes looking after people. It has been observed earlier in the present book that caring for others may well be a chosen role for *some* people. Thus, we may ask whether some people 'just are' kind and selfless while others 'just are' selfish or limited. Should we blame Joseph Roth's character Theodor Lohse in *The Spider's Web*, a novel we will discuss next, for being obnoxious, should we blame Harriett Frean for being 'blind' and limited?

The thrust of the argument of this book is that people *can* learn to develop autonomy and to navigate inter-personal relations in such a way as to improve human flourishing as a whole. Perhaps this is not so? Perhaps it is 'of the nature of things' that some individuals succeed in flourishing while others 'perish as though they had never been'? Perhaps some individuals are so 'intrinsically flawed' (whatever that means) that they will lead unhappy and unsatisfactory lives? The multiple 'influences' on every life are in fact so bewilderingly *myriad* that we can never know?

This novel illustrates very well the futility of imposing or following moral principles which do not arise from and/or are not grounded in a truly sympathetic awareness of the feelings and experiences of others. If one cannot appreciate the pleasure of another to whom one gives a gift, why do it?

Surely it is *cold* to follow moral principles merely because they are moral principles, whereas it is *warm* to appreciate their basis in the feelings of others. This is what is wrong with Kant's notion of 'duty' and the categorical imperative (in his *Groundwork of the Metaphysics of Morals*); taking no account of individual tastes and preferences, it involves only the chilly imposition of a very general (and hence useless?) 'law': as Lawrence A. Blum points out in *Friendship, Altruism and Morality*.

We juggle constantly, and unavoidably, with the 'demands' or needs of individuals, and the indifferent application of general rules of conduct. The businessman who asks his secretary to send his wife a bouquet of flowers for her birthday, is likely to find his 'generosity' less appreciated by his wife than if he had gone to the trouble of going to a florist and choosing them himself.

The Life and Death of Harriett Frean shows this point very well. The child Harriett is merely disappointed to sacrifice her doll to another, and to give up a cake at a party. She takes no pleasure in the (possible) pleasure of the recipients.

Likewise, her 'sacrifice' of Robin to her friend Priscilla turns out badly, so she might as well not have bothered?

Of course, one can never guarantee a successful outcome to the assertion of autonomy. As has been argued in Part Two, 'tempered altruism', taking account of the natures of the recipients, is more likely to result both in the retention of self-worth by the donor and, hopefully, pleasure for the recipient. We get it wrong much of the time, but sometimes we do succeed. The recipient is touched by the thoughtfulness of the donor, the donor is pleased to have given pleasure: surely a warmer experience?

RESENTMENT AND LOYALTY:

Joseph Roth, *The Spider's Web*

At first reading, Theodor Lohse, the protagonist of Joseph Roth's novel *The Spider's Web* (1923), may seem only an obnoxious individual, self-seeking, consumed by envy and resentment, anxious to make a mark for himself in any way he can. The context in which he finds himself certainly seems to be conducive to his ambition – the first part of the twentieth century in Germany, where Fascism is on the rise and young men are encouraged to embrace militaristic anti-Semitic sentiments and to join organisations that foster them. The notorious (subsequently shown to be fraudulent) *Protocols of the Elders of Zion* are distributed to all military cadets to fan the flames of distrust and loathing of Jews. (On the subject of *The Protocols*, see Norman Cohn's study, *Warrant for Genocide.*) Oaths of loyalty are sworn by the cadets to reinforce their obedience to the values current in their context.

The title *The Spider's Web* is telling:

> He thought of that spider from his boyhood days, which he used to feed each day with captured flies. He remembered waiting breathlessly as the creature climbed its web, how it watched for a second before making its final deadly rush, which was assault and in one deadly movement.
>
> He himself now sat like that, ready for the attack, determined to spring. He hated these people, without knowing why, but fabricated his own reasons for hating them. They were socialists, without a belief in a Fatherland, traitors. They were in his power ...
>
> (*The Spider's Web*, tr John Hoare, Granta Books, p25)

Thus, Theodore casts himself as the spider in this drama, but, ironically, he could equally be seen (by the reader) as a *fly*, caught in the sticky web of the *zeitgeist* (predominant current ideas and values), where 'determinants' beyond his knowledge and control are making *him* the victim of his times.

Roth was prescient about the rise of Fascism; we, the readers, can see, with the 'benefit' of hindsight, that he was all too sadly right. Let us look at two notions with relevance to this novel: Loyalty and The Spirit of the Times.

Loyalty

We have already seen in Chapter Three that the notion of Loyalty *binds* individuals to one another through either a sharing of interests or goals, or a putting aside by an individual of their own aim (if they have one!) in favour of that of another/others. In both cases, there may be a loss of autonomy. A possibly unfair and unkind characterisation of the appeal of loyalty (sometimes reinforced by acts of allegiance and promises of fidelity) is that it is a means of putting some backbone into the spineless! Certainly the comfort and security of 'belonging' reduces the sense of loneliness and vulnerability, especially for those who are uncertain about their own identity and their place in the context in which they find themselves. 'Tougher', 'independent' individuals (*as* individuals) may not be attracted by the concomitant loss of their independence that professions of loyalty involve. For Theodore, the flashy appeal of a military uniform or the sense of exclusiveness of belonging to a secret organisation with grand-sounding aims, are irresistible to such a weak character. Membership of this sort gives him a sense of power over those he fears and loathes.

However, in spite of Roth's account, it is important to acknowledge that not all communal activities should be viewed in this negative light. Sometimes individuals are powerless, *as* single individuals, to change their (often intolerable) circumstances, and can *only* do so by combining with others of like mind to do so. The Trades Union movement is surely a far more positive example of this, where a long and difficult struggle (ongoing?) has resulted in 'workers' forcing more acceptable conditions from often reluctant or unwilling 'bosses'.

The Spirit of the Times (*Zeitgeist*)

This present book does not normally concern itself explicitly with the social and political dimensions of human experience. However, some reference is frequently made to unknown and unknowable 'determinants' operating on individuals in the context of the Free Will/Determinism debate.

It has been suggested by Hegel amongst others, that there is some universal 'spirit' which manifests itself as the predominant ideas and values of a given age and sometimes called ideologies, and that this 'influences', often in undetected ways, the way people live.

The term *Zeitgeist* is frequently used, sometimes trivially to refer merely to 'passing fashions', sometimes more seriously to refer to the predominant ideas and values of a given age, with the use of the German term giving it seemingly more gravitas.

However, it is often difficult, if not impossible, to know what *counts* as the predominant ideas and values of a given age *at the time*. As Hegel has also pointed out:

"The owl of Minerva spreads her wings only with the falling of the dusk' – which is taken to mean that it is only with the benefit of hindsight that we can understand what those predominant ideas really were. (G.W.F. Hegel, *Philosophy of Right*.) In any case, what is 'a given age', and *where* are we talking about and whose ideas and values are we referring to?

Perhaps only historians can answer these questions 'when the dust has settled' and a thoughtful analysis made of the many and diverse factors contributing to such understanding?

Of what relevance is this to our reading of Roth's novel? We feel that we can see *now* the ominous rise of Fascism in Germany because we know of its horrible outcome, *but at the time* Germany was trying to recover from its disastrous experience of WW1, so that any set of ideas which aimed to reinstate the dignity of the Fatherland was likely to be attractive, at least to those individuals uncertain of their own values and aims. It has been observed that 'cream and scum rises', and that, given the 'right' circumstances (eg political system) scum *will* rise and predominate.

Roth presents Theodore Lohse as definitely representative of 'the scum', of the 'type' who always have been and always will be attracted to the trappings of showy power because they are weak, resentful and stupid. The institutions for this rise were in place and he joined them with enthusiasm.

Thus, we might say that Lohse has no alternative but to follow the pathway or trajectory that he does. But is this so? We know that very different ideas and ideals were available at the time (Communism, for example) and in fact he encounters certain of them, but these lacked the glamour of the military and similar groups; also, to individuals like Lohse there was the conflation of Communism with Jewishness fuelled by virulent anti-Semitism.

The author, Joseph Roth, was Jewish, and we can only sadly record the course of events which finally led to the horrors of the Third Reich. Certainly, not everyone did espouse their foul values but our protagonist did. With the benefit of hindsight, we may now say that he should *not* have done so, that people don't *need* to go along with the *Zeitgeist*, however strong it is, and in every age there are independent spirits who resist it and follow their own pathways, however hazardous that may be.

We may ask if there is any real difference between an 'excuse' and a 'good reason' for individuals doing what they do. Is it part and parcel of an individual's personality that they *must* do what they do? This brings us back, yet again, to the question of whether individuals have 'real' choices, or merely the illusion that they do; a question underlying all the discussions of this book, and one which can perhaps never be resolved?

AN EXPLORATION OF ALTERITY:

Charles Morgan, *The River Line*

Charles Morgan's novel *The River Line* (1949) (and play (1952)) has a rather more complex structure than the previous two books discussed, employing as it does a frame narrative, or story within a story. The main events in France during the Second World War are related later by one of the participants to someone who has not been involved in them, although other members of the original group are also present.

After seventy years since its publication, *The River Line*, which was both a successful novel and play at the time, may indeed seem rather contrived – various 'mysteries' seem artificial, and the structure of a plot-within-a-plot unnecessarily complicated. However, leaving aside these caveats to which attention will be drawn from time to time, the work does highlight a notion which has already been discussed in Part One Chapter Two, with reference to 'the self', and that is *alterity* (the radical otherness or heterogeneity of the other). I have borrowed the term from Emmanuel Levinas but put my own 'spin' on it, in order to give an example of the difficulty, if not impossibility, of 'knowing' others, in the sense of 'getting it right' – a correct appraisal of them, rather than a seriously faulty (or even fatal) one. It is shown in graphic detail in this novel.

If we dissect the main story, set during WW2, from the frame story, set much later, the main points are as follows:

Four airmen (Philip Sturgess, Julian Wyburton, 'Heron' and Dick Frewer), shot down over German-occupied French territory, one (Sturgess) American, the other three British, are involved in the River Line, an escape route for such as themselves. In charge of the River Line is Marie, a Frenchwoman. The acute danger in which they find themselves is well portrayed – they do not know one another but they have been thrown together by their circumstances. They are understandably jumpy and nervous, in constant fear of detection by the Germans, and this reinforces their wariness of one another, because betrayal is a constant feature of these escape lines, particularly as a result of the 'planting' of an agent provocateur, pretending to be a fellow escapee. This type of situation is portrayed in surely at least a dozen other novels, films and TV series.

Thus the scene is set for their suspicion of 'Heron' (so nicknamed by them because of his birdlike appearance), and this is fuelled by a number of incidents: Heron is fluent in German and chats at unnecessary length (in their view) to German soldiers they encounter; he steals stamps from a safehouse; he offers to accompany Marie, whose father Pierre is rabidly anti-German because of his own past experience, on a dangerous mission where Sturgess and Wyburton fear that Heron will betray her.

Finally, after furtive discussions of their suspicions, they decide Heron must be killed, and they kill him. Were they right to do so? The reader may think so, given the acute circumstances in which they were enmeshed. Could they have been mistaken about Heron? Was he in fact what he appeared to be, a loyal British airman, anxious to escape from occupied France in order to rejoin the British forces, and continue the fight against the Germans?

We find out in the 'frame story' which unfolds around the main story, and relates the subsequent meeting of the protagonists some years after the end of the war, and while the pieces fall into place rather too neatly, it does provide 'proof' that Heron was indeed innocent, and that their killing him was unjustified.

For our purposes, it is not necessary to go into detail about the rather creaky unwinding of the Heron 'mystery', and we may now doubt whether finding out that Heron was the brother of a well-to-do respectable English girl, Valerie, is any guarantee of his innocence. Spies and traitors come in all shapes and sizes (eg Anthony Blunt and Kim Philby), including apparent 'pillars of the Establishment', as recent history has shown.

Today's readers may wonder why on earth the four men didn't chat to one another in spite of, or even because of, their restricted situation, volunteer something about their pasts, their families, military experiences and so on, but the explanation is surely that men of that age and class did *not* volunteer such information; they were much more *formal*. Nowadays, people *do* chat to one another far more, although as Feminists have pointed out, *men* find it more difficult to do so and often prefer to limit the subject matter of their chatting to their hobbies and sports rather than 'personal' matters!

We may ask whether this does in fact solve the problem of penetrating the alterity and apparent opacity of others, and the answer may be *to some extent*, for it surely enables individuals both to understand *themselves* (by trying to do so through their conversing with others) and indeed also to understand others, if the process is reciprocated. But only *if* – and we have seen in our discussion of selfhood that myriad 'techniques' are still available to us for concealment of the fragile and vulnerable self: we deceive ourselves because we do not understand ourselves, and because we fear and/or dislike what we reveal to ourselves; likewise, we may present to others a more favourable picture than we know 'in our heart of hearts' to be a more accurate one. And others may well be doing the same to us!

How often do not people present themselves in as favourable a light as possible; stressing a rather grander background than they have, emphasising that they have been to a 'good' university, and maintaining that their job/profession is more important than it is. Poses and masks abound and are widespread to protect the fragile, shivering, vulnerable self from 'invasion' and damage.

Perhaps the events in France recounted in *The River Line* are merely an extrapolation of what normally occurs between individuals seeking to, yet wary of, communicating with one another? It is an extreme situation in extreme circumstances but, nonetheless, may serve to highlight the problems facing all such efforts at communication, and also what may be involved in making life-or-death decisions about how to *act* towards one another, some of which *do* occasionally occur even in 'normal' life. The quotidian is dotted with such pitfalls and minefields, and we surely do well to proceed cautiously in our interaction with others.

Thus, the main issue illustrated by this novel is the impenetrable otherness of others, how it is difficult, if not impossible on some occasions, to form an accurate picture of others, of how one can get it horribly wrong with tragic consequences. This problem can be more intense in a situation where the view one has of another's personality and actions crucially *matters*, as it does in *The River Line*.

EXPANDING HORIZONS AND ALTERNATIVE WORLDS:

Pascal Mercier, *Night Train to Lisbon*

Interestingly, while we hear a good deal about the Fascist regimes of Germany, Italy and Spain in fact, fiction and film, there is little about the equally loathsome regime of Salazar from 1933-74 in Portugal. *Night Train to Lisbon* (2004), a novel by Pascal Mercier, the pen-name of Swiss Professor of Philosophy Peter Bieri, does something to put the matter right, set, as it largely is, in Fascist Portugal. (A film version of *Night Train to Lisbon*, directed by Bille August, appeared in 2012.)

Thus the protagonist of the novel, and possibly the reader, know little about this regime, and learn a great deal more about it as the story unfolds.

The protagonist, Raimund Gregorius, a middle-aged lecturer of 'dead' languages (ancient Greek, Latin and Hebrew) in a gymnasium in Bern, highly respected by his colleagues and pupils although affectionately nicknamed 'Papyrus' behind his back, begins a life-changing journey after a chance encounter with a Portuguese girl on a bridge near his place of work. Much is made in the novel of the metaphor of short-sightedness – Gregorius is very short-sighted but his trip to Lisbon improves not only literally his eye-sight, thanks to an optician he meets there, but also his 'seeing' a great deal more of life than he has hitherto experienced.

After his impetuous departure to Lisbon, caused by his encounter with the Portuguese girl, and especially with the Portuguese *language* and a book by a Portuguese writer, Amadeu de Prado, he begins to trace Amadeu and meets friends of his and, most importantly, his sister Adriana, who has remained loyal to his memory to a disturbingly excessive extent, preserving his room and possessions with an obsessive intensity.

The horrors of the Salazar regime slowly emerge. Amadeu was a doctor who saved the life of a hated secret policeman known as 'The Butcher of Lisbon', to the disgust of the citizens of the city. Gregorius meets a former friend of Amadeu, Jorge O'Kelly, a talented pianist whose hands have been crippled by the secret police, and hears of a girl with whom Amadeu has been involved and whose life he has saved by taking her away from Lisbon when she was in danger of discovery.

Gregorius learns more about Amadeu when he visits an elderly monk, Father Bartolomeu, who taught the doctor when he was a schoolboy.

Two general points can be made, the first a) concerning 'expanded horizons', the second b) concerning the features of the 'Actual' and the 'Possible Non-Actual'.

What is to be learned from this novel? Certainly, what is well portrayed is the contrast between the 'chilly' cosiness, stability and safety of Switzerland and the warm but unstable and dangerous Southern atmosphere of Portugal, and one sees Gregorius' personality expanding because of the contrast. His fascination with Amadeu de Prado's personality and writing is a little more difficult to appreciate. Certainly, Amadeu de Prado was an unusual, reflective individual and his life had been richer than Gregorius', but his writings and musings, maunderings, even, do not seem particularly profound or interesting; although a speech he gave at the university was bold and dangerous, shocking his conservative father, with whom he had a somewhat vexed relationship – not uncommon between fathers and sons. As for Amadeu's relationship with his sister, this was not an uncommon one in past times where women tended (all too readily) to unquestioningly admire their more highly educated brothers and settle for becoming their 'assistants', rather than exhibiting any autonomy of their own. It should be pointed out that this was far from unusual – educational opportunities were not available to women except in exceptional cases, so they had no alternative but to assume subsidiary roles vis-à-vis more highly qualified men.

In addition to this, Adriana has another reason for her devotion to her brother, and this is that he saved her life when she choked, by doing an impromptu but successful tracheotomy.

It remains difficult to understand quite why Gregorius is so fascinated by Amadeu, except that, having hitherto led a very narrow and unadventurous life himself, visiting a very different country and learning of a very different life from his own has opened up all manner of undreamed of possibilities to him, though not necessarily possibilities he would wish to actualise for himself. As was observed at the beginning of this discussion, very little is generally known about Portugal and the Salazar regime, and this is for both Gregorius and the reader of the novel a source of intriguing interest, and may account in part for the popularity of the novel. In the film version, Jeremy Irons makes a creditable stab at the part of Gregorius, managing to portray the effect of new experiences on a dusty academic.

Perhaps, in the end, the 'moral' of this novel is to recommend an openness to alternative possibilities or possible worlds, and to a consideration, at least, of whether or not they *could* be actualised. Individuals locked in their own trajectories may never consider alternatives, although this may not be because *they* have chosen the trajectory but because it is 'as it were' chosen *for* them, or rather, they just find themselves following it blindly and unreflectively.

Has Gregorius acquired greater autonomy from his experiences? The running metaphors of improved eye-sight and of the warmth of the South contrasted with the cold of the North, do something to suggest this. Certainly, Gregorius' *sympathies* are engaged by hearing about Amadeu's life, and may indeed point to some sort of turning point for him.

b) Alternative worlds: the 'Actual' and the 'Possible Non-Actual'

In Part One Chapter One the two levels of consciousness, the actual and the possible-non-actual, have been introduced, and it has been suggested that the actual is experienced through perceiving, and the possible-non-actual through imagining, although the experience of the actual is interwoven with imagining; a sustained act of imagining giving rise to eg a novel produces a possible-non-actual *world*, 'peopled' by, but not identical with, the subject matter and events resembling those of the actual world.

In the novel under discussion, Pascal Mercier, perhaps because he is a Professor of Philosophy, has produced a multi-layered work of imagining in which several alternative worlds interpenetrate with one another: that of Bern and that of Portugal, which are experienced *as actual* by Gregorius as he moves between them, but which we the reader experienced as possible-non-actual through our own act of imagining. There are also the PNAWs of Amadeu's life and writings, experienced *by* Gregorius as possible-non-actual – Amadeu is no longer alive – Gregorius *imagines* them. These are more structured examples of the rather *un*structured longings and yearnings we all have 'to be somewhere else' (usually the country, by the sea, in the south of Europe) as an antidote to our probably boring and tedious lives. But such yearnings often lack detail; the good novelist (or poet) can fill them in and enrich such sketchy attempts.

The great advantage of Literature (or any good writer's account, although 'historical' accounts are arguably less 'immediate') is that states of affairs and events are 'frozen in time', which means that the reader can return to them again and again: they lack the evanescence of experience of the actual world. PNAWs (Possible Non-Actual Worlds) continue to 'exist' for as long as we are prepared to explore them; but it is a *different mode of existence* from that of the Actual World; as has been pointed out in Part One Chapter One.

While we may agree with Jean-Paul Sartre in *Imagination: A Psychological Critique* that *imagined* subject matter has an 'essential poverty' in that no further details are available over and above what is described, we can 'embroider' it at will, if we so choose, with our own imaginings even though there is nowhere to go for authentication of them, as may be available with historical accounts if, for example, new documents 'come to light'. (See also L.C. Knights' 'How Many Children Had Lady Macbeth? An Essay in the Theory and Practice of Shakespeare Criticism' (1933), included in *Explorations*, New York UP, 1964.) But does this matter? The term 'free-ranging' is often applied to imagining and this is surely its *advantage* over accounts subject to procrustean requirements of truth, validity and authentication.

The wilder shores of Fantasy and Science Fiction demonstrate how far it is possible to extrapolate from the rigidity of Actual World experience.

Given 'free rein' as it is in works of literature (and painting and music), imagining is constrained only by the requirement of 'intelligibility' and that is a very flexible one; many works of literature etc (especially poetry) operate on the fringes or borders of intelligibility, sometimes crossing them into a bewildering area of hints, clues and speculation.

This is the area in which consciousness is at its most blatantly *creative*, but, as I have been at pains to point out, *all* the activities of consciousness are creative insofar as they incessantly try to 'make sense of' their constantly 'changing-over-time' subject matter. Consciousness is a maelstrom of activity, structuring and restructuring its own subject matter in an attempt to 'make sense of things'. We classify, and reclassify, impose rules, amend rules and so on in the light of new experience. At any point of 'stopping the clock', we might be able to say how things seem '*now*', but '*now*' has already gone into the past.

The presentation of the PNAWs of literature, fiction and poetry, not only demonstrates the creativity of the writer but also encourages or even provokes the creativity of the *reader* to both 'fill in the gaps' in the text and to relate the subject matter of the text to their actual experience, their understanding (always unstable!) of the Actual World.

Too much concern with the 'Truth' or Authenticity of what is presented in literature can be inhibiting to such creativity; requirements of 'the practical' and 'the physically-possible' can present stumbling blocks to considering what *might* be possible and even *might be* made actual.

7

POETRY

MEMORY AND NOSTALGIA:
John Betjeman, *Collected Poems*

In Part One Chapter One, remembering has been cited as one of the activities of consciousness, whose subject matter is PNAWs, but PNAWs of what has been actual at some time *for* the individual, and only *that* individual, although some aspects may be shared with others because they have been contiguous, though not identical in space and time. At least some aspects of the individual's Actual World experience can be 'brought to mind', and 'relived', though there may be no means available to authenticate their accuracy. Memory is notoriously unreliable! Many things which have happened actually to the individual are forgotten, others *mis*remembered and sometimes embroidered to their advantage. Pithily put by William Shakespeare, *Henry V*, Act 4 Scene 3: 'Old men forget and shall be forgot but he'll remember with advantages what feats he did that day!'

Furthermore, at least in the view of some theorists (such as Freud and his followers), some memories are repressed or suppressed inaccessibly, although they may still be 'affecting' the individual's conscious behaviour in disturbing ways.

Nonetheless, unreliable or not, the ability to 'access' the PNAWs by remembering enriches the individual's Actual World experience, and inability to do so eg in the case of Alzheimer's disease, is found to be tragic not by the individual concerned, at least in its severe stages, but by those who knew them.

Similarly with all works of literature, though perhaps rather more 'scrappy', memories are 'fixed in time', available for reconsideration as long as the individual can remember them. Older people have increasing recourse to them (sometimes to the exasperation of younger people!) as their actual experience slows down, but surely this is an invaluable source of expanding human experience as a whole? Recent experience of the Coronavirus pandemic and its enforced stasis on whole populations has resulted in the excavations of many memories of World War Two as comparisons are made between the two, so that restrictions and hardship are 'put into perspective'. Grandchildren hear for the first time, and with attention unlikely to be given under 'normal' circumstances with their activity-filled situations, of the travails and hardships of their grandparents eighty years earlier.

Nostalgia

Closely related to remembering, perhaps a 'subsection' of it, is *nostalgia*, the essence of which is a warm, often sentimental, feeling towards the remembered subject matter: certain of the individual's past experiences, and sometimes a wistful yearning to *return* to such experience; the sense that what has actually happened *in the past* was better than their present experience, and a regret that it cannot be retrieved and 'lived again' in *actual* experience. Such nostalgic longings usually air-brush out the more unpleasant or painful aspects of the memories concerned!

With these general reflections in mind, let us consider the poet in question.

John Betjeman (1906-84) has been, and possibly still is, one of the most popular and widely read English poets. This popularity sometimes results in disparaging dismissal by more 'serious' literary critics/theorists but, in spite of that, there is acute observation of the mores of a particular period in English history, that of Betjeman's own life, which will evoke many echoes in those who have lived through that period, a time when full-blown consumer Capitalism as we now know it had not taken over, mainly because of the austerities of World War Two and its aftermath when 'consumer goods' were just not available, and the English class system still held considerable sway.

Betjeman's place or role in this comes over very clearly in his poetry. Being 'posh' (a member of the aristocracy, or in an upper middle class profession – the Church, the Military, the Law, Oxbridge) was *de rigueur*, while being 'in trade', or for that matter Jewish or 'foreign', was not! Betjeman's father was 'in trade', running a factory making fashionable household furniture and objects, and furthermore, the family had German origins, not desirable in a country with two wars between Germany and Britain – one in Betjeman's childhood and the other during his adulthood. In spite of not having the right background, Betjeman passionately loved all things English – the Anglican church, Victorian architecture, and married into the (minor) aristocracy himself in a perhaps desperate bid to 'belong': well documented in the Bevis Hillier biographies.

Furthermore, and perhaps strangely, he did not want things to *change*. He loathed post-war activities by Town Councils, and made fun of women taking jobs (see 'Business Women'), and longed, probably mistakenly, for a return of the *status quo, ante-bellum*, because this was (is) probably a seductive illusion, leaving out the *dis*advantages of the state of affairs for which he had a nostalgic yearning.

Nonetheless, because of his brilliant ability to evoke those 'lost times', older English readers will recognise many of his references as having been part of our own youth, and to household names of products, eg Drene shampoo, Windsmore scarf, Bravington ring, etc. But perhaps this is indeed mostly so for those people approximately contemporaneous with Betjeman's life; perhaps they make no sense to younger people, or to foreigners, but then one could say the same about, for example, many of the references in Shakespeare, which is why there are so many 'glossaries' of Shakespeare's terminology. Why should there not be one for Betjeman?

Many English people have a rose-tinted nostalgic view of an England which probably never actually existed – an orderly, stable society, hierarchical in a supposedly non-threatening way, where sheep safely graze, the ploughman plods his weary way, the vicar greets his parishioners at the door of an ancient church set in an idyllic yew-filled churchyard (also filled with mute inglorious Miltons), and there is always honey for tea when the clock stands at ten to three! We don't want to think about dark Satanic mills, child labour, and all the horrors of the industrial revolution, and the exploitative aspects of the British Empire.

Thus, John Betjeman is full of contradictions, many of which he recognised himself and laughs at – the 'idyllic' Cornish holidays with 'Sand in the sandwiches, wasps in the tea' ('Trebetherick'); the class snobbery which excluded him from total acceptance in English society, however hard he tried to ignore it; his fear of death, despite his religious beliefs:

> Dr Ramsden cannot read *The Times* obituary today
> He's dead ...
>
> *– Collected Poems*, John Murray, 2006, p166

Other aspects include his very poignant sensitivity to loneliness and old age, and to the desperation of small children (as in 'Archibald' and 'Hertfordshire').

Betjeman's taste for 'big sporting women' is particularly well portrayed in a poem such as 'A Subaltern's Love Song':

> We sat in the car till twenty to one
> And now I'm engaged to Miss Joan Hunter Dunn.
>
> *– Collected Poems*, p88

He knows it is rather absurd, but lets us know that he thinks so too.

His 'ear' for catchy rhythms makes so much of his verse memorable and repeatable, an aspect sometimes derogated by 'the serious', but this is what makes his poetry so popular and memorable – the pithy, witty encapsulation of serious issues in a few brief lines.

Betjeman's desperate climbing into acceptance into society, largely achieved because he became 'a National Treasure' (exemplified by the statue of him in London's St Pancras Station) was always an uneasy one with which he was not entirely comfortable. Radio and television did a great deal to enhance his reputation (his TV documentary on 'Metroland' is particularly delightful), and his championing of the rescue of the Euston Arch endeared him to 'preservationists'. The combination of his poetry and his delightful personality seems likely to ensure that he will be long remembered, and may prompt reinforcement of the importance of remembering, for catching the mores, values and aspirations of a given age, which we can revisit again and again, should we wish to do so. It may also inspire readers to revisit, re-order and reflect upon their own memories, and to disentangle nostalgia from a more sober charting of their own past experience, access to which may be extended and corrected by the experience and writings of others.

CONVERSATION, PROCLAMATION, MONOLOGUE:

T.S. Eliot, *The Family Reunion*

In Part Two, Chapter Four, we have explored the notion of conversation and suggested that it could take a number of forms, dependent on the aims of those involved, but of which they are sometimes unaware. In my discussion of *The River Line*, I have argued that the *situation* which is recounted brings to the surface the metaphysical question of *Alterity*.

Just as the exceptionally acute *situation* presented in *The River Line* serves to draw attention to the question of alterity, both the situation *and* the formal verse-drama form of *The Family Reunion* serve to highlight some problems about the notion of *conversation*. I have observed that the different types of conversation frequently intermingle with one another; many or all of them might be present in any interchange of any length, and disentangling them for the purposes of analysis (should one be so inclined) can be quite a task!

While *speech* is the *main* means of communication between individual humans – a transferring of the individual's thoughts, views, feeling etc to another – it is almost always accompanied/supplemented by physical gestures, facial expressions, the performing of small tasks to help (or hinder) the other. Those quite rare individuals who do not employ these supplements are found disconcerting and puzzling to others. While the suggestion that if eg 'Italians had their arms tied behind their backs, they would be unable to speak' may be just a witty exaggeration, it makes the point about the importance of gesticulation.

In performances of the play, the deadpan formal way of speaking stresses the *absence* of gesticulation and becomes proclamation rather than conversation. The characters externalize their thoughts and preoccupations with little attempt to communicate them to others, or any concern with whether they are doing so.

Proclaiming rather than conversing is surely an element often found in 'ordinary' conversation and may be due only to social awkwardness on the part of the speaker or else a sense of self-importance which makes the speaker unconcerned with whether or not they are communicating with others. The situation sparks off such externalizations but there seems to be no real desire to hear or explore the responses of others to it.

In *The Family Reunion* a number of serious and important matters are at issue but we largely learn only of the responses to them of the individual characters.

Part of one speech (of Agatha's) is worth quoting at some length because it surely encapsulates the difficulties of communication, in spite of attempts to do so:

> Thus with most careful devotion
> Thus with precise attention
> To detail, interfering preparation
> Of that which is already prepared
> Men tighten the knot of confusion
> Into perfect misunderstanding,
> Reflecting a pocket-torch of observation
> Upon each other's opacity
> (...)

– 'The Family Reunion',
The Complete Poems and Plays, Faber, 1969, p290

We have already discussed alterity – the impenetrable otherness of others, and here is another way of talking about it – the difficulty of 'knowing' another, of penetrating their opacity when, indeed, we can do no more than shine a pocket-torch of observation upon them.

In Chapter Four I have contrasted negative or destructive conversation with positive or constructive conversation, the first aiming to 'win an argument' or 'get at the truth', rather than to encourage participants to express their own thoughts and views, however fumblingly and haltingly. While the first has its place (especially when practical decisions have to be made and implemented), the second surely enriches the range of 'what can be said about' some state of affairs, however 'wrong' and 'dotty' it may appear, as a means of encouraging unique individuality and enlarging the pool of possible ways of looking at and articulating human experience as a whole.

The Family Reunion starkly illustrates the deficiencies of attempts at communication – the various characters and groups of characters do little to communicate with one another, locked as they are into their own preoccupations, although there is perhaps *some* advance in interpersonal understanding in the exchanges between Agatha and Mary when family secrets are exposed.

Furthermore, I have suggested that the 'indirect therapy' of attending to a matter *other than* the individual's direct worries and concerns may be a means of avoiding premature medical 'treatment'. The cliché of 'clearing the air' may go some way to characterizing this, although, as the sceptical will point out, it may generate more heat than light!

Is this what has happened in *The Family Reunion*? Perhaps, because the official occasion for the gathering is Amy's birthday but it is also the occasion for those attending, if not to converse with one another, at least to externalize their preoccupations, and this appears to bring about some sort of *resolution* of 'the family curse', represented, rather cryptically, by the Eumenidies.

Written and first presented in 1939, Eliot's verse drama explores the interaction between the members of a family who have come together to celebrate both the matriarch's birthday and the return of the long-absent son, Harry.

Eliot makes effective use of the dramatic form to give two sets of 'voices' which alternate to stress the dislocation between those characters (Amy, Harry, Agatha, May) who are centrally concerned with the main 'plot' (ie the return of Harry; the mysterious disappearance of his wife on an ocean liner; family tensions, long buried but brought to the surface by his return) and another set of characters (Ivy, Violet, Gerald, Charles) who are concerned only with surface, quotidian matters (eg the pending arrival of Harry; listening to the News) and who are bewildered and uncomprehending about the central drama unfolding before them. They do *not* understand what is going on. The formality of the speech reinforces this dislocation and makes it chillingly amusing, but also gives it a deadly effectiveness. A family curse, never fully explained, hovers over the entire play, which may or may not have been 'defused' at the end.

A key character, Agatha, a lecturer in a women's college, has been absent for much of the drama but, or perhaps, because of her absence, has a better grasp of what is involved than any of the other characters. *Lack* of communication, so well captured by another playwright, Harold Pinter, in a quite different way, is paramount. Secrets are suppressed, half-explained, buried, given a quite different interpretation, accusations made, and this captures the tumult of many attempts at communication of important matters. The characters talk, or rather, proclaim, to one another but they do not *listen* to one another, or if they do, they fail to *understand* what is being said.

The play could be seen as a succession of monologues, addressed, if to anyone, to the audience, rather than as a number of dialogues between the characters. Each character externalises her/his preoccupations and view of the situation in which they find themselves, making a bizarre unsettling mosaic of the family reunion refracted through the prism of each member's response to it.

Eliot's declamatory style is very well suited to this; more 'natural' conversation would not be so effective for conveying the *lack* of communication which may underlie more seemingly 'normal' exchanges where each individual probably fails either to express adequately what they are trying to say, and also fails to make any 'real' contact with the other(s). Is this too gloomy a picture of individuals' attempts to 'reach' one another? Perhaps much of the time it doesn't matter; enough warmth is generated to ease the individual's isolation, at least on a surface level. We have seen in our discussion of conversation in Chapter Four, that many things are going on, many games being played, when individuals try to talk to one another and, at least at the practical level, things need to be decided or things *done* before it may be too late!

But we have also seen that two minds, much less 'great minds', do *not* think alike, because of the unique individuality of each mind. One could even put it that *no* two minds think alike. Attempting to express this unique individuality, as suggested by SeC2, merely reinforces this separation, even if it enriches the pool of possible human experience. It may be 'interesting' but perhaps also 'isolating'?

The pressure to find 'common ground' is very great. We *generalise* by finding *shared* characteristics or properties of the subject-matter of our experience, and we could not function without doing so: thus uniquely individual aspects are ignored, as Nietzsche points out in '*Origin of the logical*'. This is particularly so when we are in 'practical mode', needing to make decisions and to act upon them, but when we are in reflective mode, there is 'time' to attend to the *differences*.

Thus Eliot's declamatory style is a half-way house to bringing these differences to the surface – we have a shared subject matter, the family reunion, but each of the characters is preoccupied with his or her own 'take' on the occasion. Nobody is *really* listening to anybody else, or only for a brief period, after which they veer off at a tangent back to what concerns each of *them*. However, stress on and noticing of difference may and should lead to an expanding of the pool of possible human experience, from which we can formulate new and varied *shared* configurations, thus enriching the realm of possibility.

PARTICULARS AND ESSENCES:

Lorine Niedecker, *Collected Works*

Uniquely particular subject matter *can* be brought to attention, and mused upon, uncluttered by practical or theoretical considerations, and this is the sphere *par excellence* of the poet.

The terms 'particular' and 'essence' are closely linked but not synonymous because 'particular' can refer to any single instance, state of affairs or object, irrespective of its significance, whereas 'essence' means the most significant or important feature. Indeed we use the term 'essence' freely to mean 'the most important feature of', and thus talk of 'capturing the essence of' (something).

There are as many 'essences' as there are individual consciousnesses to focus on them and find them important, and, if they are so disposed, by talent or inclination, to try to *record* them both for their own satisfaction and for the consideration of others to whom they are communicated. *This* surely is poetry.

Hitherto unnoticed details are 'separated out' from their surroundings and given prominence, 'seen afresh'; marginalia can be brought to the centre of attention and displace what has hitherto been considered important or significant.

The poetry of Lorine Niedecker has a wide range of subject matter but we will concentrate on the ways in which some of her poems illustrate the central questions of particularity and essence.

It has been suggested that there are as many 'essences' of subject matter as there are individual consciousnesses to experience it, but that this unique particularity may become blurred and lost (or never *found* in the first place) in the generalising nature of our attempts to understand the world and ourselves. But, by saying so relatively little in most cases, compared with the plenitude of prose or of general conversation, poetry may do something to bring this unique particularity to our attention.

A unique 'take' on a seemingly insignificant event becomes memorable, for example in "I knew a clean man ... ":

(...) He

wades the muddy water, fishing,
falls in, dries his last pay-check
in the sun, smooths it out
in *Leaves of Grass*. He's
the one for me.
                    – *Collected Works*, University of California Press, 2002, p208

The seemingly tiny incident of drying and smoothing the last pay-check, by being given prominence, conveys the importance of the man to the poet. We learn from biographical sources that in fact he becomes her husband! Thus, this incident, because so recorded, becomes as it were the essence of him, as the minutiae of daily life sometimes do for individuals.

In *reflective mode* we 'stop the clock' as it were, and lift out a section of Actual World experience for our atemporal consideration, or rather we replace the temporality of the Actual World with the Possible Non-Actual World's own internal temporality. This is so if we are reflecting *on* the

Actual World, if the Possible Non-Actual World is presented to us directly, as in a poem: the clock-stopping and lifting out are not needed. We can enter straight into the Possible Non-Actual World in question. This may well be running in parallel with Actual World states of affairs and events, but we are *attending* to those of the Possible Non-Actual World.

In the poem under discussion, 'I knew a clean man ... ', there is minimal information – an anonymous man who may or may not be a professional fisherman, and probably impoverished, falls in the water and then is concerned to preserve a wet pay-check (cheque). Why does he make such an impression on the poet so that 'he's/ the one for me'? So sparse is 'background information' that the reader can only reflect, perhaps, upon the way in which seemingly slight occurrences/events can make a memorable and lasting impression.

Again and again with Niedecker the reader is or may be intrigued by the conjunction of the *economy* of what is stated with the richness of the *implied* but unstated resonances it engenders. The 'space'/'room' of such PNAWs allows this imaginative input – there is no limit or boundary to prevent such considerations.

Of course, there is always room in any imaginative work for *alternative* readings or understanding – we may disagree with the political or moral stance of a nineteenth century novel (and the tendency towards secular preaching, eg as in George Eliot), however convincingly argued, or propose alternative stances which are diametrically opposed to those proposed. *A fortiori*, in poetry there can be *far more* room for alternative readings because there is so little subject matter to get in their way – as paradoxical as this might sound. The borderline between intelligibility and *un*intelligibility can be a very hazy one, difficult to draw or else constantly shifting.

In some of Lorine Niedecker's poems we are given more initial information because the subject matter is *named*, ie Thomas Jefferson, Charles Darwin and William Morris: Americans and Europeans are likely to have a working knowledge of the latter two, but Europeans perhaps not of Jefferson, even if his name is familiar. Nonetheless, tiny details of their lives not usually stressed – Jefferson's migraines, Darwin's love of music – enrich our understanding of them.

It has been suggested that Niedecker concerns herself with the 'marginalia' of famous people's recorded lives, rather than focusing on what is most widely known about them. (See for example Elizabeth Willis, 'Who Was Lorine Niedecker?', where she refers to Niedecker's 'attention to the periphery'(https://poets.org/text/who-was-lorine-niedecker, retrieved 30/ 11/20). If this is so, how do we decide which is which, or what contribution to our understanding (of the person) is made by drawing attention to 'marginalia'?

We have already observed that 'lifting' the seemingly insignificant from the larger context can *give* it significance and even present it as the 'essence' of the subject matter, an 'essence' hitherto never recognised as such.

There can be plenty of 'room' or 'space' in the PNAWs of poetry for readers to 'fill in' with their own imaginative input. The term 'resonance' captures what may be *suggested* but not stated or claimed. There is considerable 'openness', and what *is* stated may be so marginal to what is normally assumed about the subject matter that new and unexpected pathways are opened up. Learning that Jefferson had '4 day migraines but ...' suggests how brave and determined he was to keep going. Is this 'the essence' of the man? No, but it is *an* essence the poet considers important and wants to draw attention to. Just as a painter may make a preliminary sketch and then fill in the detail, so the sparseness of poetry (the *absence* of detailed information) gives the reader a preliminary sketch on which to reflect.

We learn from biographical information about Lorine Niedecker that she lived a quiet, relatively uneventful life in fairly straitened circumstances in Wisconsin, a rural water-bound area of the USA very much bound up with *water*, and the ways of life of those to whom it is very present and important: fishing; dealing with flooding; its flora and fauna. Her circumstances were indeed far from wealthy, sometimes positively impoverished, so that she had to take menial jobs such as cleaning in order to survive, especially when her deteriorating eyesight forced her to give up her job as a librarian. However, she did not despair and, as her poetry shows, retained the ability to notice and write about small but significant matters in her life and environment (as well as her reading) which held her attention. One might say that the sparseness of her life and the sparseness of her poetry mirror one another. A noting of *particulars* is certainly very prominent in her work, but without labouring the point about them – it is up to the reader to find and follow the resonances.

The poem 'My Life by Water' makes it clear that Lorine Niedecker regarded water as *part* of herself, part of her make-up, perhaps *her* essence? People sometimes claim to be 'at one' with their context, that their surroundings have contributed to their make-up. Just as usual, unfortunately, is the claim that individuals feel 'out of tune' with their surroundings, and either persist unhappily *in* them, or seek to escape from them, and sometimes succeed in doing so. This is part of what makes up an individual's unique particularity.

In this poem, written in the late 1960s, some of the minutiae of a life by water are sparsely mentioned: there is no elaboration but there is enough information to convey to the reader both its day-to-day aspects ('Muskrats/ gnawing/ doors', 'Rabbits// raided/ my lettuce') and the more aesthetic qualities, those likely to be attended to by those who are not that close to its more mundane realities. And there are some brief, evocative and innovative conjunctions:

> thru birdstart
>   wingdrip
>   weed-drift

> – *Collected Works*, pp237, 238

The title is suggestive: could it mean that Niedecker's life was 'written' by water, as it were? Water was such a *dominant* feature of her life, after all. But could water be seen in some sense as the *author* of her life, as a writer is the author of a poem or novel? It is far from an unusual idea to suggest that individuals are *formed* by their setting or context but the appositeness of Niedecker's implying that her life was formed / determined / written by water makes the point with striking brevity or economy – the writer is herself *written*, and in turn *writes* that this is so. At the same time, she both *writes* and is *written*, is *writing* and being written.

While it could possibly be said that *all* individuals are being written all the time by their contexts, not all of them are actively conscious that that is so; it takes a writer both to be aware of it, and to point it out!

The ceaseless creative activity which is consciousness, operating through the unique individual, will unavoidably produce unique individual responses to experience, but these often go unnoticed, are blurred by the urge to 'get on with things', to make practical decisions, to formulate *some* plausible account of 'the nature of things', however ramshackle, threadbare and unoriginal.

As any teachers worth their salt know, the most seemingly dim and unpromising pupil/student may produce startling, exciting articulations in the right sympathetic setting/context, if they are encouraged to make the effort, however stumbling at first, as we have discussed in Chapter Four.

It may be objected that this attitude is, to say the least, unsettling and even disruptive and anarchic, because running in parallel with encouragement and enjoyment of the innovative, is an equally strong desire for certainty and permanence, hence the constant search for *Truth*, or The Truth; but as a quick glance or (better) a measured perusal of human history demonstrates, notions of 'Truth' and 'the Truth' constantly change willy-nilly – the creative and innovative constantly break through or rupture the iron bands of what once appeared to be 'written in stone', and sabotage any hope of real, unalloyed permanence.

KALEIDOSCOPE AND MOSAIC:

David Miller, *Spiritual Letters (Series 1-5)*

If we stop the clock or freeze in time a kaleidoscopic succession of individual experiences and record them in writing, we have something resembling a mosaic, or perhaps a tapestry. Components are recognizable but their combination gives a rewarding 'picture' or whole. But this is only if the record in words is well done, otherwise the end product may be of no interest to the observer/reader.

To extend, and possibly strain, the metaphor further, initial bafflement about what one is 'seeing' may be likened to being 'on the wrong side of the tapestry' (or the underside of the mosaic if that were possible) where there is only an unintelligible tangle of threads, or pieces of ceramic; seen from the 'right' side, the picture becomes clear and full of interest to the beholder.

These preliminary remarks give us an entrée into *Spiritual Letters*, because the style in which they are written is completely appropriate.

David Miller's writing differs considerably from that of either John Betjeman or T.S. Eliot or even Lorine Niedecker. It is prose poetry, of which David Miller himself writes:

> ... the prose poem in English is curiously ignored or distrusted, on the one hand, and yet practised by a wide range of significant poets, on the other. Those who ignore or distrust it often have a conviction – or prejudice – that poetry can only be poetry when it's in verse, or if you dislike that term, when it's written in lines. Alternatively, they identify the prose poem as a peculiarly French form of poetic writing.
>
> – 'Close-up: The Prose Poem',
> *Poetry News: the newsletter of The Poetry Society*, Winter 2003/4, p4

He also mentions Thomas Traherne (1636-1674), who, like David Miller, wrote both in prose and in lines, and whose prose poetry might be compared with *Spiritual Letters*.

David Miller agrees that many features of 'traditional' poetry may be present in the prose poem, and also that 'it is comparatively easy for the prose poem to move towards other forms of writing, such as the story, the diary or the essay.' ('Close-up: The Prose Poem.')

This may well be so but nonetheless, the first reaction of many readers of the *Spiritual Letters* may be one of complete bafflement – to whom are they addressed? Who are they about? Where and when are they set? Why 'spiritual', why 'letters'? No person, place or time is *named* (or at least with very few exceptions); we are given no guidance as to how to 'get into' them, and may be inclined to dismiss them as 'unintelligible'. But this would be a mistake because, with an effort of careful reading, there are great riches to be found in the mosaic-like structure of the *Letters*, fragmentary and unfocused as they may seem on first acquaintance.

They are episodic, full of what might be considered as non-sequiturs, moving from one piece of subject matter to another without explanation, and appearing to 'speak' with many voices, not only the author's, and are interspersed with a number of quotations, the source of some of which is given in the endnotes. The multi-vocal aspect of the letters suggests Mikhail Bahktin's notion of *polyphony*. Occasionally, there is a more recognisable poem-in-lines, although its relation to its context is often obscure.

Are there any underlying themes to be found? In my view, there are several which persistently recur which may perhaps be seen as agonies and ecstasies, the former more striking and frequent than the latter. Could we say that the *Letters* as a whole are called 'spiritual' because they express a preoccupation with a search for meaning – making sense of human existence – both in and beyond the here and now, ie in terms of transcendence. Certainly the sad, tragic, violent, transitory features of human existence are very thoroughly presented, the brevity of the episodes or incidents making them that much more poignant. We wish to know more at the same time as we avert our gaze. Loneliness, isolation, loss, cruelty, suffering, incomprehension and misunderstanding are expressed again and again like a nagging toothache.

Two passages from the *Letters* illustrate the sensibility involved:

> Heavy rain falling on the table and chairs, the potted plants and flowers, the long grass and boards. Two magpies and a crow, moving back and forth through the leaves of the trees. He received in the mail a map of a city area, without any notations or accompanying letter. Black outlines of tar, rectangular: glistening on the pavement. A fragment of bone in a white cup on the table. He woke in pain, in a strange room; glancing in the bedside mirror, he saw that his face was bruised and streaked with blood. Someone writes on the stones, another taps on them with a stick. When my friend and I visited the old poet, he told us of what he'd seen during the war, what he'd gone through. I was writing a poem in his honour – drafting a second version – when the ringing of the phone woke me. She had hung sheets of black plastic over the shelves, covering all of the books.
>
> – *Spiritual Letters (Series 1-5)*, Chax Press, 2011, p47

> (...) On the ceiling, gold flowers arranged in straight lines and circles, and gold rectangles. He got out of bed in the night, feeling ill, and fell on the stairs and lay there helplessly, with no one in earshot, and died. We wandered through the snow in the cemetery until we found the old Cabbalist's grave, surrounded by broken glass. Later that afternoon, in another cemetery, we saw the graves of writers and artists, snow falling faster, heavier. *Darkened windows, candle-light and battery torches, sirens and the army on every corner ...* – Where did you think your friends had disappeared to, he asked, when they never called or answered your calls again? The woman still denied knowing about the deportations and deaths, angering him further. *I saw a ladder of tremendous height made of bronze, reaching all the way to the*

heavens, but it was so narrow that only one person could climb up at a time. To the two sides were fastened all sorts of iron instruments, as swords, lances, hooks, and knives; so that if any one went up carelessly he was in great danger of having his flesh torn ... She dreamt that she was eating curds, and woke with a sweet taste still on her tongue. *I at once told this to my brother, and we realized that we would have to suffer, and that from now on we would no longer have any hope in this life.*

– Spiritual Letters (Series 1-5), p84

The *Letters* may sometimes appear as merely the private associations of ideas of their author. There is a relentless succession of the fractured worlds of meetings, partings, deaths and loss, puzzling, upsetting, bizarre encounters, nocturnal walks and drinks in bars, hospital visits... deathbeds.

The poet and critic Michael Thorp, in his book *A Shared Inherence,* spoke of 'shards' in the *Letters*; I slightly prefer the word 'splinters', but both words convey the sharpness, fragmentariness of the *aperçus*. But the fragments *do* come together in the end to make a mosaic of a particular individual's (ie David Miller's) apprehension of the world of his experience, pessimistic though it frequently is, a sensitive and compassionate individual, despairing of human folly, cruelty, and insanity or craziness.

In some ways, David Miller's pessimism resembles Schopenhauer's, although for rather different reasons, and *expressed* very differently: Schopenhauer the philosopher, identifies the constant welling up of unsatisfied desires as a source of suffering; Miller charts *individual* instances of suffering and pain, which are all the more poignant as a consequence.

However, intermingled with the sad and disturbing episodes, making up a 'tragic' vision, are many 'lighter' elements: friends are valued, though they often die or lose contact, as are children and animals, colour and form in nature and architecture, and painters and paintings are constantly noted. In a world of unhappiness, moments of some relief are to be found.

Thus with *Spiritual Letters* we have a detailed record, written over twenty years or so, of the significant experiences of *one* unique individual's, the author's, singular trajectory, while ranging over other material as well (to do with history, art, religion etc). The reader may have a sympathetic response to all the sad and tragic fragments presented while perhaps wishing that there had not been quite so many of them ... At the same time, the reader may be delighted by the striking *aperçus*, the brief insights into the natural world, architectures, visual vignettes and the joys of friendship.

This is *one* record of a succession of significant experiences, amongst other things, and while noting that it is not 'simply' a diary or even a memoir, but rather something more 'constructed', as well as varied in texture and in reference, surely each and every individual, had they the time, inclination and talent, *could* produce their own record of what has been significant in their own unique trajectories, but this does not usually happen, if at all, apart from the brief and intermittent, disorganized accounts in conversation with others, or explored privately by remembering. Systematic or involved and organised presentations are normally the preserve of the writer or raconteur, while the 'vapour trails' of countless other individuals dissolve in the air, although fragments or resonances of these may remain in the experience of others. But here there is surely no reason why many other individuals should not at least *try* to record their unique perceptions of their lives over a number of years, thus adding to the sum total of human literature.

(For another reading of the *Letters*, see Keith Jebb, 'David Miller, *Spiritual Letters*', *Golden Handcuffs Review*, No 26, 2018/19.)

At bottom, every high degree of caution in making inferences and every skeptical tendency constitute a great danger for life. No living beings would have survived if the opposite tendency – to affirm rather than suspend judgment, to err and *make up* things rather than wait, to assent rather than negate, to pass judgment rather than be just – had not been bred to the point where it became extraordinarily strong.

> – Friedrich Nietzsche, 'Origin of the Logical', *The Gay Science*,
> tr Walter Kaufmann, Vintage Books, 1974, pp171-2

Catalogue Sonnet

I am determined by my class
I am determined by my sex
I am determined by my God
I am determined by my genes
I am determined by my unconscious
I am determined by my childhood
I am determined by my death
I am determined by my climate
I am determined by my homeland
I am determined by my work
I am determined by my newspaper
I am determined by my deep linguistic structures
I am determined by my etcetera
I am determined to be free

> – Anthony Rudolf, *European Hours: Collected Poems*,
> Carcanet, 2017, p75

There, nothing but order and beauty dwell,
Abundance, calm and sensuous delight.

> – Charles Baudelaire, '*Invitation to the Voyage*',
> tr Richard Stokes,
> *https://digitalcommons.chapman.edu/cgi/*
> *viewcontent.cgiarticle=1749&context=music_programs*, retrieved 3/1
> 2021)

CONCLUSION

THE DISCUSSIONS OF THIS BOOK HAVE presented an account of human experience in terms of *how it feels* to possess consciousness. As individuated, embodied, sensate entities experiencing a number of activities of consciousness, desiring and imagining stimulate us to take an interest in ourselves and in our context, try to make sense of it, and try to find our way about in it in order to survive.

Such is the bewildering bombardment of stimuli from the incessant creativity of consciousness, that we desire to find certainty and fixity, but if we do, it is inevitably temporary and open to revision because of the temporality of our experience. Our descriptions and explanations are constantly subject to change.

Throughout our discussions, mention has been made of the vexed question of whether or not we can 'really' formulate choices and purposes to bring about their resolution, or whether we are just the vehicles of unknown and unknowable 'determinants' which 'have their own agenda', and which we are powerless to affect. Has the script been written elsewhere so that we are 'merely players'? The answer is that we can *never* know, but, because all our experience is predicated on the assumption that we can, at least, initiate and direct what we do, either our deliberations and agonizings have some point, or life would be meaningless, an invitation to descend into despair.

Thus, we can only proceed *as if* we have *some* control over our lives, that we can take responsibility for them, and that it may be possible to recalibrate and improve how we live, although it could be that such adjustment and recalibration goes on 'automatically', as is suggested by Damasio's intriguing notion of 'socio-cultural homeostasis', an analogue to physical homeostasis.

In order to do so we need to recognize certain deep-seated, ineliminable *tensions* within consciousness, most particularly that between the desire for autonomy (to follow unique individual trajectories) and the desire to belong with others, thus alleviating our loneliness and vulnerability.

We also need to recognize and access the richness of possible worlds, available to us through imagining, especially the highly-structured ones of Literature, and to make consideration of them a *central* feature of our experience rather than an optional extra; a position to which they are unfortunately sometimes relegated. A consideration of *alternative* states of affairs to those of the actual world should surely be an ongoing feature of our deliberations. Our ability to move freely between the three levels of consciousness enables us to experience a far greater range of subject matter than if we attend only to the *actual*.

Because we are living, sensate, embodied entities which *feel*, we can never eliminate *suffering* from our experience – there will always be terrible accidents, natural disasters, and horrible diseases; people will die, but surely many of the crasser sorts of suffering resulting from cruelty and callous indifference could be reduced, so that more attention could be given to *felicity*, to the sheer enjoyment of much of life, rather than to our 'sinfulness' and inadequacy.

I have suggested that our always problematic interaction with one another might be improved in a climate which encourages the expression of *unique* apprehensions of 'the nature of things' which can be fed into the pool of human possibility, and on occasion actualized so that unique trajectories are not prematurely stifled and blocked: so that we *flourish* rather than *perish*.

While the vapour trails of the unique trajectories of countless individuals may be evanescent in the extreme, remembered only by those who have been close to them (in the sombre words of Samuel Wesley, 'and some there be which have no memorial, who are perished as though they had never been') – those of some remarkable individuals persist in the collective human memory, especially if they are recorded, and can serve as a source of inspiration (or a terrible warning!) to future generations.

I have also suggested that premature and total flight into transcendence through drugs or religious experience should be recognized as denying much of human potential (although it will always remain an option for some), because it can involve the amputation of much of our worthwhile lived experience, as well as being an abdication of responsibility for attempting to improve our earthly existence, transient though it necessarily is.

While the improvement of communicating has been urged, there might well be a role for periodic withdrawal from our busy chatter-filled world, for periods of *silence*, in which we reflect on and reorder our thoughts and ideas about our lives and our relations with others, for a clarification and reassertion of selfhood, rather than its *denial*. Secular retreats: for the non-religious; analogues of monastic or religious retreats, but without the rigours of monastic life, such as cold cells, hard beds, frugal food and praying on cold stone, where physical discomfort has perhaps been overvalued?

–Thus, a celebration of 'earthly delights' alongside a reduction of avoidable ills, could make our existence on earth less 'a vale of tears' than one in which the incessant creativity of consciousness makes it possible that we come closer to where, in Baudelaire's words (in Richard Stokes' translation):

> ...nothing but order and beauty dwell,
> Abundance, calm and sensuous delight.

SELECT BIBLIOGRAPHY

Anand, Paul. *Happiness Explained: What Human Flourishing Is and What We Can Do to Promote It*, NY; Oxford: OUP, 2016.

Aristotle (384-322 BC). *The Ethics of Aristotle: The Nicomachean Ethics*, tr J A K Thomson, revised by Hugh Tredennick, Harmondsworth: Penguin, (1976) 1979.

Atterton, Peter, Matthew Calarco and Maurice Friedman, eds. *Levinas and Buber: Dialogue and Difference*, Pittsburgh, PA: Duquesne UP, 2004.

Bakhtin, M M. *The Dialogic Imagination: Four Essays*, ed Michael Holquist, tr Caryl Emerson and Michael Holquist, London; Austin, TX: University of Texas Press, 1981 (first published in Russian, 1975).

Barry, Peter. *Beginning Theory: An Introduction to Literary and Cultural Theory*, 4th ed, NY; Manchester: Manchester UP, 2017.

Barry, Peter. *Reading Poetry*, NY; Manchester: Manchester UP, 2013.

Baum, William M. *Understanding Behaviorism: Behavior, Culture, and Evolution*, 3rd ed, Malden, MA; Oxford; Chichester: Wiley, 2017.

Bayne, Tim, Alex Cleeremans and Patrick Wilken, eds. *The Oxford Companion to Consciousness*, NY; Oxford: OUP, 2009.

Bayne, Tim. *The Unity of Consciousness*, Oxford: OUP, 2010.

Bazalgette, Peter. *The Empathy Instinct: How to Create a More Civil Society*, London: John Murray, 2017.

Berlin, Isaiah. *Two Concepts of Liberty*, Oxford: Clarendon Press, 1961; incorporated in: *Four Essays on Liberty*, Oxford: OUP, 1969.

Betjeman, John. *Collected Poems*, London: John Murray, (1958) 2006.

Black, Max. *Models and Metaphors: Studies in Language and Philosophy*, Ithaca, NY: Cornell UP, 1962.

Blackmore, Susan. *Consciousness: A Very Short Introduction*, NY; Oxford: OUP, 2005.

Bloom, Paul. *Against Empathy: The Case for Rational Compassion*, NY: Ecco Press, 2016.

Blum, Lawrence A. *Friendship, Altruism and Morality*, NY; Abingdon, Oxford: Routledge, (1980) 2009.

Boden, Margaret A. *AI: Its Nature and Future*, NY; Oxford: OUP, 2016. (Reprinted as *Artificial Intelligence: A Very Short Introduction*, OUP, 2018.)

Boden, Margaret A. *Mind as Machine: A History of Cognitive Science*, NY; Oxford:

OUP, 2006.

Brown, Geoffrey. *Minds, Brains and Machines*, Bristol: Bristol Classical Press, 1989.

Browne, E Martin. *The Making of T.S. Eliot's Plays*, London; Cambridge: CUP, 1969.

Bruner, Jerome. *Actual Minds, Possible Worlds*, London; Cambridge, MA: Harvard UP, 1986.

Buber, Martin. *I and Thou*, tr Ronald Gregor Smith, 2nd ed, Edinburgh: T & T Clark, 1958 (first published in German, 1923).

Caruso, Gregg D, ed. *Exploring the Illusion of Free Will and Moral Responsibility*, Plymouth, Devon; Lanham, MD: Lexington Books, 2013.

Cascardi, Anthony J, ed. *The Cambridge Introduction to Literature and Philosophy*, NY; Cambridge: CUP, 2014.

Casey, Edward. *Imagining: A Phenomenological Study*, Bloomington; London: Indiana UP, 1979.

Cassam, Quassim. *Self-Knowledge for Humans*, NY; Oxford: OUP, 2014.

Chappell, Timothy. *Knowing What to Do: Imagination, Virtue and Platonism in Ethics*, NY; Oxford: OUP, 2014.

Coplan, Amy and Peter Goldie, eds. *Empathy: Philosophical and Psychological Perspectives*, NY; Oxford: OUP, 2011.

Coxhead, David and Susan Hiller. *Dreams: Visions of the Night*, London: Thames and Hudson, 1976.

Crook, John H. *The Evolution of Human Consciousness*, Oxford: Clarendon Press, 1980.

Dainton, Barry. *The Phenomenal Self*, NY; Oxford: OUP, 2008.

Damasio, Antonio. *The Feeling of What Happens: Body and Emotion in the Making of Consciousness*, London: Heinemann, 2000.

Damasio, Antonio. *Self Comes to Mind: Constructing the Conscious Brain*, NY: Pantheon Books / London: Heinemann, 2010.

Damasio, Antonio. *The Strange Order of Things: Life, Feeling, and the Making of Culture*, NY: Pantheon Books, 2018.

Davies, Martin and Glyn W Humphreys, eds. *Consciousness: Psychological and Philosophical Essays*, Oxford: Blackwell, 1993.

Dennett, Daniel C. *Consciousness Explained*, London: Allen Lane The Penguin Press, 1992.

Dennett, Daniel C. *From Bacteria to Bach and Back: The Evolution of Minds*, London:

Allen Lane The Penguin Press / NY: Norton, 2017.

De Waal, Frans. *The Age of Empathy: Nature's Lessons for a Kinder Society*, NY: Harmony Books, 2009.

Dunne, J W. *An Experiment with Time*, London: Faber, (1927) 1958.

Dreyfus, Hubert L. *What Computers Still Can't Do: A Critique of Artificial Reason*, Cambridge, MA: The MIT Press, 1992 (rev ed of *What Computers Can't Do*, 1979).

Eldridge, Richard, ed. *The Oxford Handbook of Philosophy and Literature*, NY; Oxford: OUP, 2009.

Eliot, T.S. *The Complete Poems and Plays*, London: Faber, 1969. (Includes *The Family Reunion*.)

Esposito, Roberto. *Persons and Things: From the Body's Point of View*, tr Zakiya Hanafi, Malden, MA; Cambridge: Polity, (2015) 2018.

Farkas, Katalin. *The Subject's Point of View*, NY; Oxford: OUP, 2008.

Forster, E M. *Howards End*, Harmondsworth: Penguin Books, (1941) 1967 (first published 1910).

Freeman, Kathleen, [tr and ed]. *Ancilla to the Pre-Socratic Philosophers*, Cambridge, MA: Harvard UP, (1947/48) 1970.

Freud, Sigmund. *The Interpretation of Dreams*, tr Anthea Bell, NY; London: Penguin Books, 2002 (first published in German, 1899).

Freud, Sigmund. *The Psychopathology of Everyday Life*, tr and ed James Strachey, NY: Basic Books, (1955) 2010 (first published in German, 1901/1904).

Frey, Jennifer A and Candace Vogler, eds. *Self-Transcendence and Virtue: Perspectives from Philosophy, Psychology and Theology*, NY; Abingdon, Oxfordshire: Routledge, 2019.

Gabriel, Markus. *I Am Not a Brain: Philosophy of Mind for the Twenty-First Century*, tr Christopher Turner, Medford, MA; Cambridge: Polity, (2017) 2019 (first published in German, 2015).

Gardner, Helen. *The Art of T.S. Eliot*, London: Faber, (1949) 1968.

Gardner, Kevin J. *Betjeman and the Anglican Imagination*, Waco, TX: Baylor UP / London: SPCK, 2010.

Glover, Jonathan. *Alien Landscapes? Interpreting Disordered Minds*, Cambridge, MA: The Belknap Press of Harvard UP, 2014.

Glover, Jonathan. *I: The Philosophy and Psychology of Personal Identity*, London: Allen Lane, 1988.

Godfrey-Smith, Peter. *Other Minds: The Octopus and the Evolution of Intelligent Life*,

London: Collins, (2016) 2017.

Goffman, Erving. *The Presentation of Self in Everyday Life*, NY; London: Penguin Books, 1990 (first published 1959).

Goldman, Alan H. *Philosophy and the Novel*, NY; Oxford: OUP, 2013.

Goleman, Daniel. *Emotional Intelligence: Why it Can Matter More Than IQ*, London: Bloomsbury, 1996.

Gregory, Richard L (ed). *The Oxford Companion to the Mind*, 2nd ed, NY; Oxford: OUP, 2004.

Hallie. Philip P. *Cruelty*, rev ed, Middletown, CT: Wesleyan UP, 1982.

Harman, Oren. *The Price of Altruism: George Price and the Search for the Origins of Kindness*, London: The Bodley Head / Vintage, 2010.

Hegel, Georg Wilhelm Friedrich. *Elements of the Philosophy of Right*, tr H B Nisbet, ed Allen W Wood, NY; Cambridge: CUP, (1991) 2017 (first published in German, 1820).

Heidegger, Martin. *Being and Time*, tr John Macquarrie and Edward S Robinson, Malden, MA; Oxford: Blackwell Publishing, (1962) 2005 (first published in German, 1927).

Heidegger, Martin. *Poetry, Language, Thought*, tr Albert Hofstadter, NY: Harper & Row, 1975.

Heller, Michael. *Conviction's Net of Branches: Essays on the Objectivist Poets and Poetry*, NY: Spuyten Duyvil, 1985 (Chapter 5: 'Lorine Niedecker: Silence and Light').

Hillier, Bevis. *Betjeman: The Bonus of Laughter*, London: John Murray, 2004.

Hillier, Bevis. *John Betjeman: The Biography*, London: John Murray, 2006.

Hills, Alison. *The Beloved Self: Morality and the Challenge from Egoism*, NY; Oxford: OUP, 2010.

Hodgson, David. *The Mind Matters: Consciousness and Choice in a Quantum World*, NY; Oxford: OUP (Clarendon Press), (1991) 1993.

Honderich, Ted. *Actual Consciousness*, NY; Oxford: OUP, 2014.

Honderich, Ted. *On Determinism and Freedom*, Edinburgh: Edinburgh UP, 2005.

Honderich, Ted. *A Theory of Determinism: The Mind, Neuroscience and Life-Hope*, NY; Oxford: OUP, 1998.

Hume, David. *A Treatise of Human Nature: Being an Attempt to introduce the experimental Method of Reasoning into Moral Subjects*, ed Ernest C Mossner, abridged edition, NY; London: Penguin Books, (1969) 1985 (first published 1739, 1740).

Humphrey, Nicholas. *Soul Dust: The Magic of Consciousness*, Woodstock, Oxfordshire; Princeton, NJ: Princeton UP, 2011.

Husserl, Edmund. *Cartesian Meditations: An Introduction to Phenomenology*, tr Dorion Cairns, The Hague: Martinus Nijhoff, 1960 (first published in French, 1931).

Illich, Ivan. *Limits to Medicine: Medical Nemesis: The Expropriation of Health*, London: Marion Boyars, (1975) 2010.

Jaynes, Julian. *The Origin of Consciousness in the Breakdown of the Bicameral Mind*, Boston, MA: Houghton Miflin, 1976.

Kafka, Franz. *The Metamorphosis and Other Stories*, tr Joyce Crick, NY; Oxford: OUP, 2009 (first German edition of *Der Verwardlung*, 1915).

Kant, Immanuel. '*An Answer to the Question: 'What is Enlightenment?'*', in *Kant's Political Writings*, ed Hans Reiss, tr H B Nisbet, NY; Cambridge: CUP, (1970) 1989 (first German edition of *Was ist Aufklärung?*, 1784).

Kant, Immanuel. *Critique of Judgement*, tr James Creed Meredith, NY; Oxford: OUP, (1952) 2007 (first published in German, 1790).

Kant, Immanuel, *Critique of Practical Reason: and other works on the theory of ethics*, tr Thomas Kingsmill Abbott, London [et al]: Longmans, Green, (6th ed), 1923 (first German edition of *Kritik der Praktischen Vernunft*, 1788).

Kant, Immanuel. *Critique of Pure Reason*, tr J M D Meiklejohn, London: J M Dent / NY: E P Dutton, (1934) 1959; tr Norman Kemp Smith, London: Macmillan, 1961 (first published in German, 1781, 1787).

Kant, Immanuel. *Groundwork of the Metaphysics of Morals*, tr Christopher Bennett, Joe Saunders and Robert Stern, NY; Oxford: OUP, 2019 (first published in German, 1785).

Kenny, Anthony. *Action, Emotion and Will*, NY; Abingdon, Oxfordshire: Routledge, (1963) 2003.

Kristjánsson, Kristján. *The Self and Its Emotions*, NY; Cambridge: CUP, 2010.

Kropotkin, Peter. *Mutual Aid: A Factor of Evolution*, London: Heinemann, 1902.

Kuhn, Thomas S. *The Structure of Scientific Revolutions*, London; Chicago: University of Chicago Press, (1962) 2012.

Küplen, Mojca. *Beauty, Ugliness and the Free Play of Imagination: An Approach to Kant's Aesthetics*, Cham, Switzerland: Springer, 2015.

Lemert, Edwin M. *The Trouble with Evil: Social Control at the Edge of Morality*, Albany: SUNY Press, 1997.

Levinas, Emmanuel. *Totality and Infinity*, tr Alphonso Lingis, Pittsburgh: Duquesne UP, [1969] (first published in French, 1961).

Lewis, C S. *The Screwtape Letters: Letters from a Senior to a Junior Devil*, London: Collins, 2012 (first published 1942).

Lodge, David. *Consciousness and the Novel: Connected Essays*, Cambridge, MA: Harvard UP, 2002.

Lewis, Hywel D. *The Elusive Mind*, London: Allen & Unwin / NY: Humanities Press, 1969.

Maibom, Heidi L, ed. *Empathy and Morality*, NY; Oxford: OUP, 2014.

Maitre, Doreen. *Literature and Possible Worlds,* London: Middlesex Polytechnic Press, 1983.

Maitre, R A. *Blue Barometers*, Liskeard, Cornwall: Peterloo Poets, 1986.

Mead, George Herbert. *Mind, Self and Society*, ed Charles W Morris, annotated edition by Daniel R Huebner and Hans Joas, London; Chicago: University of Chicago Press, 2015 (first published 1934).

Mercier, Pascal. *Night Train to Lisbon*, tr Barbara Harshav, NY: Grove Press, 2008 (first published in German, 2004).

Merleau-Ponty, Maurice. *Consciousness and the Acquisition of Language*, tr Kenneth Silverman, Evanston, IL: Northwestern UP, 1979 (first published in French, 1964).

Merleau-Ponty, Maurice. *The Phenomenology of Perception*, tr Donald A Landes, NY; Abingdon, Oxfordshire: Routledge, 2012 (first published in French, 1945).

Miller, David. *Art and Disclosure: Seven Essays,* Exeter: Stride Publications, 1998.

Miller, David. *Spiritual Letters (Series 1-5)*, Tucson: Chax Press, 2011; *Spiritual Letters,* London: Contraband Books, 2017.

Morgan, Charles. *The River Line*, London: Robson Books, 1988 (first published 1949).

Nagel, Thomas. *Equality and Partiality*, NY; Oxford: OUP, 1991.

Nagel, Thomas. *The Last Word*, NY; Oxford: OUP, 1997.

Nagel, Thomas. *Mind and Cosmos: Why the Materialist Neo-Darwinian Conception of Nature is Almost Certainly False*, NY; Oxford: OUP, 2012.

Nagel, Thomas. *Mortal Questions*, Cambridge; NY: CUP, 1979.

Nagel, Thomas. *Other Minds: Critical Essays 1969-1994*, NY; Oxford: OUP, 1995.

Nagel, Thomas. *The Possibility of Altruism*, Princeton; Chichester: Princeton UP, 1978.

Nagel, Thomas. *Secular Philosophy and the Religious Temperament: Essays 2002-2008*, NY; Oxford: OUP, 2010.

Nagel, Thomas. *The View from Nowhere*, NY; Oxford: OUP, 1986.

Nagel, Thomas. *What Does It All Mean? A Very Short Introduction to Philosophy*, NY; Oxford: OUP, 1987.

Niedecker, Lorine. *Collected Works*, ed Jenny Penberthy, London; LA; Berkeley: University of California Press, 2002.

Nietzsche, Friedrich. *The Gay Science: with a prelude in rhymes and an appendix of songs*, tr Walter Kaufmann, NY: Vintage Books, 1974 (first published in German, 1887).

Nussbaum, Martha C. *Anger and Forgiveness: Resentment, Generosity and Justice*, NY; Oxford: OUP, 2016.

Nussbaum, Martha C. *Creating Possibilities: The Human Development Approach*, Cambridge, MA: Harvard UP, 2011.

Nussbaum, Martha C. *Love's Knowledge: Essays on Philosophy and Literature*, NY; Oxford: OUP, 1990.

Nussbaum, Martha C. *Political Emotions: Why Love Matters for Justice*, Cambridge, MA: Harvard UP, 2013.

Nussbaum, Martha C. *Upheavals of Thought: The Intelligence of Emotions*, Cambridge: CUP, 2001.

O'Neill, Onora. *Acting on Principle: An Essay on Kantian Ethics*, NY; Cambridge: CUP, 2013.

O'Shaughnessy, Brian. *Consciousness and the World*, NY; Oxford: OUP, 2000.

O'Shaughnessy, Brian. *The Will: A Dual Aspect Theory*, (2 vols), 2nd ed, NY; Cambridge: CUP, 2008.

Parfit, Derek. *On What Matters*, NY; Oxford: OUP, 2011.

Parfit, Derek. *Reasons and Persons*, NY; Oxford: OUP, 1984.

Penberthy, Jenny, ed. *Lorine Niedecker: Woman and Poet*, Orono, ME: National Poetry Foundation, 1996.

Polanyi, Michael and Harry Prosch. *Meaning*, London; Chicago: University of Chicago Press, 1975.

Priestley, J B. *Man and Time*, London: Aldus Books, 1964.

Ricoeur, Paul. *Freud and Philosophy: An Essay on Interpretation*, tr Denis Savage, New Haven: Yale UP, 1970 (first published in French, 1965).

Ricoeur, Paul. *The Rule of Metaphor: The Creation of Meaning in Language*, tr Robert Czerny with Kathleen McLaughlin and John Costello, SJ, [NY]; London: Routledge, (1978) 2003 (first published in French, 1975).

Ridley, Matt. *The Origins of Virtue: Human Instincts and the Evolution of Cooperation*,

London: Penguin Books, 1996.

Robinson, Howard. *From the Knowledge Argument to Mental Substance: Resurrecting the Mind*, NY; Cambridge: CUP, 2016.

Robinson, Marilynne. *Absence of Mind: The Dispelling of Inwardness from the Modern Myth of the Self*, London; New Haven: Yale UP, 2010.

Ronen, Ruth. *Possible Worlds in Literary Theory*, Cambridge: CUP, 1994.

Rorty, Amélie Oksenberg, ed. *Explaining Emotions*, London; LA; Berkeley: University of California Press, 1980.

Roth, Joseph. *The Spider's Web*, tr John Hoare, London: Granta Books, 2004 (first published in German, 1923).

Rousseau, Jean-Jacques. *On the Social Contract*, tr G D H Cole, Dover Publications, NY, 2003 (reprinted from the J M Dent edition, 1913; first published in French, 1762).

Rudolf, Anthony. *European Hours: Collected Poems*, Manchester: Carcanet Press, 2017.

Ryle, Gilbert. *The Concept of Mind,* London: Hutchinson, 1949.

Sartre, Jean-Paul. *The Imaginary: A Phenomenological Psychology of the Imagination*, tr Jonathan Webber, NY; London: Routledge, 2004 (first published in French, 1940).

Sartre, Jean-Paul. *Imagination: A Psychological Critique*, tr Forrest Williams, Ann Arbor: The University of Michigan Press, 1962 (first published in French, 1936).

Sartre, Jean-Paul. *Huis Clos and Other Plays*, tr Stuart Gilbert and Kitty Black, NY; London: Penguin Books, 2000 (first French edition of *Huis Clos*, 1944).

Sartre, Jean-Paul. *Sketch for a Theory of the Emotions*, tr Philip Mairet, London: Methuen, 1962 (first published in French, 1939).

Scheler, Max. *The Nature of Sympathy*, tr Peter Heath, NY: Archon Books, 1970 (first published in German, 1923).

Schiller, Friedrich. *On the Aesthetic Education of Man*, tr Keith Tribe, London: Penguin Books, 2016 (first published in German, 1794).

Schliesser, Eric, ed. *Sympathy: A History*, Oxford: OUP, 2015.

Schopenhauer, Arthur. *Prize Essay on the Freedom of the Will*, ed Günter Zöller, tr Eric F J Payne, NY; Cambridge: CUP, 1999 (first German version, 1839).

Schopenhauer, Arthur. *The World as Will and Representation*, tr E F J Payne, (2 vols), NY: Dover Publications, 1966 (first published in German, 1818, 1844).

Schutz, Alfred. *The Phenomenology of the Social World*, tr George Walsh and Frederick Lehnert, Evanston, IL: Northwestern UP, 1967 (first published in German, 1932).

Searle, John R. *The Rediscovery of Mind*, London; Cambridge, MA: The MIT Press, 1992.

Sinclair, May. *The Life and Death of Harriett Frean*, London: Virago, (1980) 2008 (first published 1922).

Singer, Peter. *The Most Good You Can Do: How Effective Altruism Is Changing Ideas About Living Ethically*, New Haven, CT: Yale UP, 2015.

Smith, Adam. *The Theory of Moral Sentiments*, London: Penguin Books, 2010 (first published 1759).

Smith, Grover. *T.S. Eliot's Poetry and Plays: A Study in Sources and Meaning*, London; Chicago: University of Chicago Press, 1974.

Staddon, John. *The New Behaviorism*, 2nd ed, Hove; NY: Psychology Press, 2014.

Stein, Edith. *On the Problem of Empathy*, tr. Waltraut Stein, Washington, DC: ICS Publications, 1989 (first published in German, 1917).

Sterne, Laurence. *The Life and Opinions of Tristram Shandy, Gentleman*, ed Graham Petrie, Penguin, (1967) 1979 (first published 1759-67).

Stocker, Barry and Michael Mack, eds. *The Palgrave Handbook of Philosophy and Literature*, Basingstoke: Palgrave Macmillan, 2018.

Strawson, Galen. *Selves: An Essay in Revisionary Metaphysics*, NY; Oxford: OUP, 2009.

Strawson, Galen. *The Subject of Experience*, NY; Oxford: OUP, 2017.

Strawson, P F. *Freedom and Resentment and Other Essays*, London: Methuen, 1974; republished: NY; London: Routledge, 2008.

Strawson, P F. *Individuals: An Essay in Descriptive Metaphysics*, London: Methuen, 1959.

Tallis, Raymond. *Enemies of Hope: A Critique of Contemporary Pessimism*, Basingstoke: Macmillan, 1997.

Taylor, Charles. *The Ethics of Authenticity*, London; Cambridge, MA: Harvard UP, 1992.

Taylor, Charles. *Sources of the Self: The Making of the Modern Identity*, NY; Cambridge: CUP, 1989.

Thomas, W I. *Social Behavior and Personality: Contributions of W I Thomas to theory and social research*, ed Edmund H Volkart, NY: Social Science Research Council, 1951.

Thomas, W I. *The Unadjusted Girl: With Cases and Standpoint for Behavior Analysis*, ed Benjamin Nelson, NY: Harper, 1967 (first published 1923).

Thornton, Mark. *Do We Have Free Will?*, Bristol: Bristol Classical Press, 1989.

Thorp, Michael. *A Shared Inherence: The Spiritual Letters of David Miller*, Berwick-upon-Tweed, Northumberland: Desert Garden Samizdat, 2005.

Traherne, Thomas. *Centuries of Meditations*, ed Bertram Dobell, London: Bertram Dobell, 1908 (written in the mid-1600s or later).

Vince, Gaia. *Transcendence: How humans evolved through fire, language, beauty and time*, [London]: Allen Lane / Penguin Random House UK, 2019.

Warnock, Mary. *Imagination*, London: Faber, 1976.

Warnock, Mary. *Imagination and Time*, Oxford: Blackwell, 1994.

Watt Smith, Tiffany. *Schadenfreude: The Joy of Another's Misfortune*, London: Wellcome Collection, 2018.

Watters, Ethan and Richard Ofshe. *Therapy's Delusions: The Myth of the Unconscious and the Exploitation of Today's Walking Wounded*, NY: Scribner, 1999.

Weber, Max. *The Protestant Ethic and the 'Spirit' of Capitalism and Other Writings*, tr Peter Baehr and Gordon C Wells, NY; London: Penguin, (2002) 2004 (first German edition of *Die protestantische Ethik und der Geist des Kapitalismus,* 1905).

Weiskrantz, Lawrence and Martin Davies, eds. *Frontiers of Consciousness*, NY; Oxford: OUP, 2008.

Wiggins, David. *Sameness and Substance*, Oxford: Basil Blackwell, 1980.

Williams, Bernard. *Problems of the Self: Philosophical Papers 1956-1972*, NY; Cambridge: CUP, 1973.

Williams, Rowan. *Being Human: Bodies, Minds, Persons*, London: SPCK, 2018.

Willis, Elizabeth, ed. *Radical Vernacular: Lorine Niedecker and the Poetics of Place*, Iowa City, IA: University of Iowa Press, 2008.

Wilson, David Sloan. *Does Altruism Exist? Culture, Genes, and the Welfare of Others*, London; New Haven: Yale UP, 2015.

Wolf, Susan... with John Koethke, *et al*. *Meaning in Life: And Why It Matters*, Woodstock, Oxfordshire; Princeton, NJ: Princeton UP, 2010.

Wrangham, Richard. *The Goodness Paradox: The Strange Relationship Between Virtue and Violence in Human Evolution*, London: Profile, 2019.

Zaehner, R C. *Mysticism. Sacred and Profane: An Inquiry into Some Varieties of Praeternatural Experience*, Oxford: Clarendon Press, 1957.

Index